KNIT YOURSELF IN

Cecilie Kaurin and Linn Bryhn Jacobsen

KNIT YOURSELF IN

Inventive patterns to tell your story in the Danish "Hen Knitting" tradition

TRAFALGAR SQUARE
North Pomfret, Vermont

First published in the United
States of America
in 2015 by
Trafalgar Square Books
North Pomfret, Vermont 05053

Originally published in Norwegian
as *Hønsestrikk til folket*.

The instructions and material
lists in this book were carefully
reviewed by the author and editor;
however, accuracy cannot
be guaranteed. The author and
publisher cannot be held liable
for errors.

ISBN: 978-1-57076-723-4

Library of Congress Control
Number: 2015948067

Photography: Linn Bryhn Jacob-
sen, Bjørn Jacobsen, Michael
Angles, Helene Svabø, Ivana
Klavis, and David Wamstad
Interior Design and Layout: Sissel
Holt Boniface, Cappelen Damm AS
Charts: Linn Bryhn Jacobsen and
Ceclie Kaurin
Translator: Carol Huebscher
Rhoades

Printed in China

Contents

Preface

Hen knitting has nothing to do with chickens, in case you were wondering. The phrase "hen knitting" was coined by the Danish author and knitter Kirsten Hofstätter forty years ago. She was disappointed that it wasn't possible to buy patterns without also purchasing the associated yarns, and so she made her own pattern book. Her patterns took a stand against the strict knitting traditions of the time. She tried to have the book published by the radical leftwing publisher Red Rooster but the book was turned down. Instead, she started her own publishing company called The Hen Press. The first knitting book was therefore called *Hen Knitting*.

Kirsten Hofstätter's knitting books have been an inspiration for everyone who likes to fantasize and design with their knitting needles without having to adhere strictly to a pattern. The term "hen knitting" came to signify knitting with colorful yarn, especially leftover yarns, particularly when the knitter designed the patterns; the garments usually featured pattern bands with motifs representing plants, animals, and people. The style symbolized the '68 generation's rebellion against the norms of the time and hen knitting was especially popular with feminists. There are undoubtedly many who still have sweaters and skirts in bright colors lying in a box in the attic.

Our goal for this book is to encourage more knitters to open up to these fun ways of knitting! Follow us at facebook.com/honsestrikk.

Creative Knitting

The point of hen knitting is to open up creativity in a simple way. That means you can choose your own colors and motifs and arrange them however you like, depending on your yarn selection. If you make a little mistake along the way, just change the project so it works out. With hen knitting, you can use yarn like colored pencils, and arrange the motifs to express your ideas. You can easily see the way forward, because you work only one pattern band at a time.

Tell a story with your garment. How do you tell a story with a sweater? Arrange the motifs to compose a story, make a statement, or show some of the garment wearer's favorite activites. You can also knit in the name of the recipient. These garments are especially fun to give to others, not to mention how nice it is to knit a garment for some-one who will feel happy wearing it!

A knitted garment is a gift with love in every stitch. If you give one away, you will warm the recipient in more ways than one.

ABBREVIATIONS

BO	bind off (British cast off)
cm	centimeter(s)
CO	cast on
in	inch(es)
k	knit
k2tog	knit 2 together
m1	lift strand between two sts and knit into back loop
m	meter(s)
mm	millimeter(s)
p	purl
p2tog	purl 2 together
psso	pass slipped stitch over
rem	remain(s)(ing)
RS	right side
sl	slip
ssk	slip-slip-knit = slip 2 sts knitwise at the same time, insert right needle into back loops and knit 2 together
st(s)	stitch(es)
tbl	through back loop(s)
WS	wrong side
yo	yarnover

YARN INFORMATION

Dale of Norway
www.dalegarnnorthamerica.com

Mango Moon Yarns
info@mangomoonyarns.com
www.mangomoonyarns.com

Ingebretsen's (Rauma too)
info@ingebretsens.com
www.ingebretsens.com

Rauma Yarn
The Yarn Guys
info@theyarnguys.com
www.theyarnguys.com

Nordic Fiber Arts
info@nordicfiberarts.com
www.nordicfiberarts.com

Rauma Ullvarefabrikk
www.raumaull.no

Sandnes Garn
Swedish Yarn Imports
PO Box 2069
Jamestown, NC 27282
800-331-5648
info@swedishyarn.com
www.swedishyarn.com
Sandnes Garn
www.sandnesgarn.no

Viking of Norway
Knitting Fever
www.knittingfever.com (use the store locator)

Du Store Alpakka
Du Store Alpakka
www.dustorealpakka.com

Hifa
Hillesvåg Ullvarefabrikk
www.ull.no

Webs — America's Yarn Store
75 Service Center Road
Northampton, MA 01060
800-367-9327
customerservice@yarn.com
www.yarn.com

If you are unable to obtain any of the yarn used in this book, it can be replaced with a yarn of a similar weight and composition. Please note, however, that the finished projects may vary slightly from those shown, depending on the yarn used. Try www.yarnsub.com for suggestions.

For more information on selecting or substituting yarn, contact your local yarn shop or an online store; they are familiar with all types of yarns and would be happy to help you. Additionally, the online knitting community at Ravelry.com has forums where you can post questions about specific yarns. Yarns come and go so quickly these days and there are so many beautiful yarns available.

Designing your own pattern

It is not difficult to design your own pattern and there are many programs you can use to make the job really fun. We have used Envisio-knit, www.envisioknit.com, which works very well for us.

When you are designing a pattern, it is important to think about the way to knit it. Long repeats, several colors in a row, and few repetitions are difficult to knit. In a garment you shouldn't have too many such patterns. On the other hand, sometimes it can be fun to see complicated motifs as they develop and the piece grows.

It is fine to have a complicated main motif but you should also balance it with some simpler, more "restful" motifs in between that will be quicker to knit.

Making patterns is one way of simplifying art— even if it's a motif with just a few stitches. Since it can sometimes be difficult to bring out a design clearly so the pattern becomes recognizable as a motif, design the most important elements first and add the rest as you go. You can also use symbolic motifs; for example, the aurora borealis can be symbolized with diagonal green and light green stripes in a panel.

Finding patterns on the internet

You can find numerous patterns on the internet and many of them are free. Several types of designs can be used; cross stitch embroidery patterns are often easy to adapt for use in knitting. If you are going to sell the garment, you must check to make sure you have permission to use the pattern.

New ways to use old motifs

In traditional hen knitting, each garment used many different colors and many different motifs. We think that you can also use hen knitting patterns in more traditional clothing and have made some suggestions about that; see, for example, the horse and hound sweaters.

Choosing yarns and colors

When you are designing your own sweater, you can get excellent help for choosing the type of yarn and colors if you have a good yarn shop in your area. The people who work there have, as a general rule, a lot of experience with what works for various garments and patterns, and they are happy to help out. If you start by thinking about what patterns and colors you want to knit with, they can suggest what types of yarn will work for your design and which colors will go well together. You will most likely find that you can't get all the colors you need from the same yarn company. In this book, there are some patterns with yarns from different mills because we couldn't find the exact color we wanted from one producer. It's a good idea to get help when substituting yarns.

For some of the sweaters in this book, unfortunately, the yarn producer has stopped making the color we used. In that case, we will suggest a similar color or an alternate color. The colors this pertains to are marked with an asterisk * in the information about the yarns for the project.

No two the same

The most fun aspect of hen knitting is that every garment is distinctive; nobody has one just like yours. Because the choice of the motifs and the arrangements of the colors are endless, the results will also be different. If you find an old hen-knit garment, see if there isn't some amusing panel that you can revive!

The designs in this book are for inspiration

The starting point is a simple basic pattern in several sizes and then you choose what patterns you like in the colors you desire. For this book, there are complete instructions for how to knit all the patterns included. But we do hope that most of you will try designing your own motifs and color combinations and not just follow the patterns in the book.

The sizes given in the patterns

Just as people come in all shapes, the shapes of the sweaters are different. Some are tight and short, some are long and wide. Check the measurements when you decide what size to make.

About Hen Knitting and the Patterns

Our book of hen knitting has an inherent contradiction, because the whole idea is to free you from lock-step patterns. When we decided to include detailed instructions, it was because we understood that many need some inspiration and a little help to get started. Don't feel that you have to follow the patterns precisely. If you think you can do something you'd like better—knit what you want. Free yourself!

Knitting in the round and cutting

All of the designs in this book are knitted in the round when you are working on the motifs, so you never have to knit color patterns back and forth. That's because we think it's quite difficult to control the stitches, pattern, and yarn when you are working on the wrong side. We have also measured how much time it took to work purl rows compared to knit rows. It took 17 seconds to make 15 knit stitches but 33 seconds to work 15 purl stitches. Not really rocket science, but we believe this shows that it really does take longer to purl. It can be exciting and scary to cut seams open when you finish the sweater, but, if you follow the step-by-step instructions in the "Cutting the armholes open" section (see page 132), it will go well.

Which pattern should I choose?

If you have a favorite basic pattern, use it. The sweaters done with T-shirt shaping in book can also be knitted with a round yoke if you make some adjustments. The top rounds after you have added the sleeves to the body in a sweater with a round yoke should be in a pattern arranged so you can easily decrease in single color rounds without disturbing the pattern. Many small panels are easiest here.

You can also use duplicate stitch afterwards, instead of knitting with three colors—see the examples of the elephants and crabs below.

The pattern didn't work!

In many of the sweaters, the pattern panels may not match the stitch count on the sleeves and body. For example, there is one tractor here that "isn't safe for driving" on the farmer's sweater.

It doesn't matter if some of the panels don't work out evenly when the elements are not very big. For most of the panels, you will also notice in the charts that we don't have full repeats for all the panels. We placed the panels together on the charts so that the best overall effect will be achieved. It doesn't mean that you should knit half a crocodile right in the middle of the sweater front. You should follow the repeats for each panel all around the body, and in the end, you might have half a crocodile at the side. It won't be very visible there.

In some of the sweaters the panels have large motifs, so only a few are needed to make it all the way around the garment. These are arranged to be closer to the top of the sweater and centered at the front. In the horse sweater, for example, we worked it out so that you won't have a sweater with half a horse.

We want to emphasize that it can often be just fine if the panels are not completely symmetrical and complete.

Help, I made a mistake!

All knitters make mistakes sometimes and don't realize it until they are several rows above the mistake. Don't waste time ripping out unless the error is so obvious that the pattern is unrecognizable. Most likely, only you will notice it and, as Arne and Carlos say, "You're not making a mistake—you're knitting a variation."

In the Beginning, There Was Helene

Cecilie's daughter, Helene, was visiting Copenhagen when she saw an amazing handknitted sweater in a display window. She thought there was something familiar about the pattern and took a photo of the sweater. "Mamma, don't you have a skirt in the attic with the same pattern—and won't you knit a similar sweater for me?"

The skirt Helen was thinking of was an old hen-knitted skirt that Cecilie had made at the end of the 1970s and had never had the heart to send to the flea market. For Cecilie, it was a memory of playing with colors and combining various panels for a fun garment that had been a delight to knit.

The old hen knitting came down from the attic, and Cecilie began work on the sweater. To make it a little more personal for Helene, who works with media and communications, Cecilie designed some bird, apple, and cell phone motif panels. The sweater was a rousing success! Helene was entirely satisfied and wears the sweater a lot. That just goes to show...

HELENE'S SWEATER—INSTRUCTIONS

Sizes	S	M	L	XL
Chest	37½ in / 95 cm	40¼ in / 102 cm	42½ in / 108 cm	45¼ in / 115 cm
Total Length	24¾ in / 63 cm	24¾ in / 63 cm	26½ in / 67 cm	27¼ in / 69 cm
Sleeve Length to Underarm	19 in / 48 cm	19¼ in / 49 cm	19¾ in / 50 cm	20 in / 51 cm

Yarn and Yarn Amounts

CYCA #4 (worsted/afghan/aran) Free Style from Dale of Norway (100% wool, 88 yd/80 m / 50 g). You can substitute yarn that knits to a gauge of 18 sts in 4 in / 10 cm.

Color Suggestions	S	M	L	XL
5651 Dark Gray	50	50	50	50
5626 Blue-violet	50	50	50	50
6015 Turquoise*	50	50	50	50
3309 Marigold	50	50	50	50
4018 Red	50	50	50	50
0010 Natural White	50	50	50	50
4617 Dark Pink	50	50	50	50
5703 Ice Blue*	50	50	50	50
5072 Dark Violet	50	50	50	50
2106 Sun Yellow	50	50	50	50
4613 Light Pink	50	50	50	50

*The original colors used for the sweater in the photo are no longer available. We've listed our suggestions for substitutes.

Needles

U.S. sizes 7 and 8 / 4.5 and 5 mm: long and short circulars and set of 5 dpn

Gauge

18 sts and 22 rnds on larger needles = 4 x 4 in / 10 x 10 cm
Adjust needle sizes to obtain correct gauge if necessary.

Sleeves

With smaller dpn and Dark Gray, CO 32 (32, 36, 40) sts. Join, being careful not to twist cast-on row. Pm for beginning of rnd. Work 16 (18, 20, 22) rnds in k2, p2 ribbing.
Change to larger size dpn and work following the sleeve chart. On the first rnd after the ribbing, increase 6 sts evenly spaced around for all sizes. Pm at the center of the underarm and move it up every rnd. *At the same time* as you work the pattern, increase 1 st on each side of the marker approx. every 5th (5th, 4th-5th, 4th-5th) rnd until there are a total of 74 (78, 82, 84) sts. Turn the sleeve inside out and work 6 rnds in stockinette for the facing, increasing 1 st on each side of underarm marker on every rnd. BO loosely. Set piece aside and make another sleeve the same way.

Front and Back (Body)

With smaller circular and Dark Gray, CO 172 (184, 196, 208) sts. Join, being careful not to twist cast-on row. Pm for beginning of rnd. Work 14 rnds (all sizes) in k2, p2 ribbing.

Sleeves

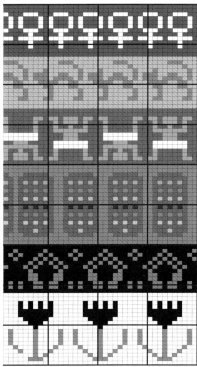

Front and Back (Body)

For Sizes L and XL, knit 10 (14) extra single-color rnds in some of the panels.

Change to larger circular and work following the body chart. For Sizes L and XL, add a total of 10 (14) extra rnds with the main color spaced over some of the panels. *At the same time*, pm at each side and move it up on every rnd. When body measures 24¾ (24¾, 26½, 27¼) in / 63 (63, 67, 69) cm, follow instructions for Finishing.

Finishing
See the Tips and Tricks on page 130. Join 23 (26, 27, 30) sts on each shoulder with Kitchener stitch. Place the back sts on smaller circular.

Neckband
Use a contrast yarn or thread to baste the shaping of the front neck. Zigzag stitch twice just below the basting and then cut away fabric above basting. Use a crochet hook to pick up and knit stitches (just below machine stitching) along the front neckline to back neck sts on each side. Make sure you have a multiple of 4 sts. With Blue-violet, work around in k2, p2 ribbing for 10 rnds. Make an eyelet rnd for the foldline: (k2tog, yo) around. Work 12 more rnds in k2, p2 ribbing and then

BO loosely in ribbing. Fold facing at foldline and sew down on WS, covering the cut edges.

Attach Sleeves
Measure the top of the sleeve and then measure half of the sleeve top width down each side of the body; pm. Machine-stitch with zigzag twice down each side of the center st for the armhole. Cut each armhole open. With facing on the wrong side of body, attach sleeves with fine back stitching. Fold facings over cut edges and sew down on WS.

Blocking
Dampen the sweater in lukewarm water. Gently squeeze out the water. Place a large towel on the floor and put sweater on top. Roll up the towel and press out excess water. Lay the sweater flat on a dry towel or on a sweater drying rack and leave until completely dry.

Onward with Karpe Diem

Chirag Patel, part of the Norwegian rap group Karpe Diem, saw Helene wearing her sweater at a concert and he thought the sweater was one of the best he had ever seen. He wanted to know where he could get one. Helene said, "You just need to tweet my mother and ask." Cecilie thought that it was fun to be asked but, although she liked Karpe Diem's music, she didn't think she needed to immediately knit a whole sweater for him without more discussion.

But he meant it seriously and some weeks later, he and Cecilie met to design a sweater for the new CD they were working on. "A cross at the neck, 10 knives at the heart and mother and father in death." Chirag had a little sketch of what children say in Norway when they really have to prove that they are telling the whole truth. For someone who didn't know much about knitting when he was growing up, it was fascinating for him to see that you can knit whatever you want in a sweater. Starting with the sketch, Cecilie designed a pattern and knitted a child's sweater as a sample. That was how the Karpe Diem sweater was created.

A Karpe Diem sweater pattern was written up, listed free on the internet, and many people knitted the design. What is most fun is that the knitters can choose their own colors so the sweater has many different variations. Ivana Klavis made one variation for her son Maximilian when he was 3 years old. Since the pattern wasn't sized, she took measurements, and, with the help of Eireen Nordlie, she made the sweater shown below. This is exactly how we had hoped people would use the patterns in this book.

Since there are many people who have asked for the Karpe Diem sweater in smaller sizes and with a round yoke, we have written it out. As an example, we used the same colors and yarn as Ivana did for Maximilian's sweater.

We have also made new styles of the Karpe Diem sweater with T-shirt shaping in 8-, 10-, and 12-year sizes + adult sizes S, M, L, and XL. The adult sweaters are in different color scheme than the original Karpe Diem sweater. In good old hen knitting tradition, we have not centered the motifs in these patterns.

KARPE DIEM SWEATER FOR CHILDREN—T-SHIRT SHAPING

Sizes (years)	8	10	12
Chest	32¼ in / 82 cm	35 in / 89 cm	37¾ in / 96 cm
Total Length	20½ in / 52 cm	21¾ in / 55 cm	22¾ in / 58 cm
Sleeve Length to Underarm	14¼ in / 36 cm	15¾ in / 40 cm	16½ in / 42 cm

Yarn and Yarn Amounts

CYCA #4 (worsted/afghan/aran) Free Style from Dale of Norway (100% wool, 88 yd/80 m / 50 g). You can substitute yarn that knits to a gauge of 18 sts in 4 in / 10 cm.

Color Suggestions	8	10	12
0090 Black	150	200	200
5621 Light Gray	150	200	200
5651 Dark Gray	150	200	200
3309 Marigold	50	50	50
0020 Natural White	50	50	50
4018 Rød	50	50	50
4826 Heather	50	50	50

Needles

U.S. sizes 7 and 8 / 4.5 and 5 mm: long and short circulars and set of 5 dpn

Gauge

18 sts and 24 rnds *on larger needles* = 4 x 4 in / 10 x 10 cm.
Adjust needle sizes to obtain correct gauge if necessary.

Sleeves

With smaller size dpn and Black, CO 36 (36, 40) sts. Divide sts evenly onto dpn and join. Work around in k2, p2 ribbing for 9 (12, 12) rnds. Change to larger size dpn and knit 1 rnd, increasing evenly spaced around to 40 (40, 44) sts.

Now work following the charted pattern for the sleeves.

Pm at the center of the underarm and move it up as you work. *At the same time* as working the pattern, increase 1 st at each side of the marker approx. every 5th (5th, 6th) rnd until there are a total of 66 (68, 70) sts.

NOTE: To have the correct length for each size, add 0 (1, 2) extra single-color rnds at the points marked by an asterisk (*) on the chart = a total of 0 (5, 10) extra rnds.

After completing the pattern, turn the sleeve inside out and knit 6 rnds in stockinette for the facing. On each rnd, increase 1 st before and after the center underarm marker. BO loosely. Set piece aside and make another sleeve the same way.

Body

With smaller circular and Black, CO 148 (160, 172) sts; join, being careful not to twist cast-on row. Pm

Sleeves, T-shirt shaping for children

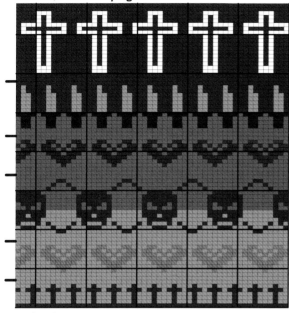

Knit 0 (1, 2) extra single-color rnds at this point

Body, T-shirt shaping for children

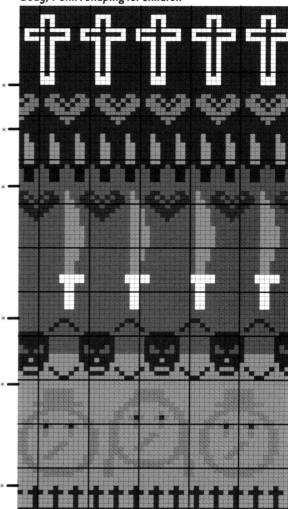

*Knit 0 (1, 2) extra single-color rnds at this point

for beginning of rnd. Work around in k2, p2 ribbing for 9 (12, 12) rnds. Change to larger circular and work following the charted pattern for the body.

NOTE: To have the correct length for each size, add 0 (1, 2) extra single-color rnds at the points marked by an asterisk (*) on the chart = a total of 0 (6, 12) extra rnds. *At the same time*, pm at each side, moving marker up as you work.

Finishing
See also Tips and Tricks on page 130.

Weave in all ends neatly on WS. Join 15 (18, 21) sts with Kitchener st for each shoulder. Place the remaining 88 sts for the neck on smaller circular.

Neckband
Pm for beg of rnd. Purl 1 rnd and then work 6 rnds stockinette, increasing 2 sts at each side = 4 sts over the rnd on every rnd. BO loosely (= facing). Fold the facing to the wrong side and sew down securely.

Attach Sleeves
Measure the width at the top of the sleeve and then measure half the total sleeve top width down each

side for the armhole. Baste line for armhole. Machine-stitch a double row of zigzag stitching on each side of the marking thread. Carefully cut open each armhole between the lines of stitching. With WS of sleeve facing on WS of body, attach sleeves with fine back stitching. Fold facing over the cut edges and sew down loosely.

Blocking
Dampen the sweater in lukewarm water. Gently squeeze out the water. Place a large towel on the floor and put sweater on top. Roll up the towel and press out excess water. Lay the sweater flat on a dry towel or on a sweater drying rack and leave until completely dry.

KARPE DIEM SWEATER FOR ADULTS—T-SHIRT SHAPING

Sizes	S	M	L	XL
Chest	37¾ in / 96 cm	40¼ in / 102 cm	43 in / 109 cm	45¾ in / 116 cm
Total Length	24¾ in / 63 cm	25¼ in / 64 cm	26 in / 66 cm	28 in / 71 cm
Sleeve Length to Underarm	19 in / 48 cm	19¼ in / 49 cm	20 in / 51 cm	21 in / 53 cm

Yarn and Yarn Amounts
CYCA #4 (worsted/afghan/aran) Free Style from Dale of Norway (100% wool, 88 yd/80 m / 50 g). You can substitute yarn that knits to a gauge of 18 sts in 4 in / 10 cm.

Color Suggestions		S	M	L	XL
	0090 Black	250	300	300	350
	6015 Turquoise*	250	250	300	300
	6135 Medium Blue*	250	250	300	300
	3309 Marigold	100	100	100	100
	0020 Natural White	50	100	100	100
	2106 Sun Yellow	50	50	50	50
	4826 Heather	50	50	50	50
	5621 Light Gray	50	50	50	50

*The original colors used for the sweater in the photo are no longer available. We've listed our suggestions for substitutes.

Needles
U.S. sizes 7 and 8 / 4.5 and 5 mm: long and short circulars and set of 5 dpn

Gauge
18 sts and 24 rnds *on larger needles* = 4 x 4 in / 10 x 10 cm.
Adjust needle sizes to obtain correct gauge if necessary.

Sleeves
With smaller size dpn and Black, CO 40 (40, 44, 44) sts. Divide sts evenly onto dpn and join. Work around in k2, p2 ribbing for 12 (14, 14, 14) rnds. Change to larger size dpn and knit 1 rnd, increasing 4 sts evenly spaced around = 44 (44, 48, 48) sts.
Now work following the charted pattern for the sleeves (see page 22).

Pm at the center of the underarm and move marker up as you work. *At the same time* as working the pattern, increase 1 st at each side of the marker approx. every 6th rnd until there are a total of 74 (76, 80, 82) sts.

NOTE: To have the correct length for each size, add 5 (5, 6, 7) extra single-color rnds at the points marked by an asterisk (*) on the chart = a total of 25 (25, 30, 35) extra rnds.

After completing the pattern, turn the sleeve inside out and knit 6 rnds in stockinette for the facing. On each rnd, increase 1 st before and after the center underarm marker. BO loosely. Set piece aside and make another sleeve the same way.

Body
With smaller circular and Black, CO 172 (184, 196, 208) sts; join, being careful not to twist cast-on row.

Sleeves, adult sizes, alternate colors

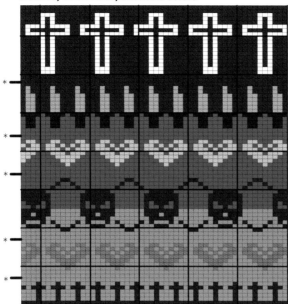

Knit 5 (5, 6, 7) extra single-color rnds

Body, adult sizes, alternate colors

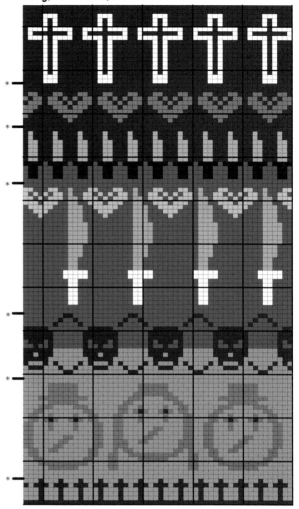

Knit 4 (4, 5, 7) extra single-color at this point rnds at this point

Pm for beginning of rnd. Work around in k2, p2 ribbing for 12 (14, 14, 14) rnds. Change to larger circular and work following the charted pattern for the body.

NOTE: To have the correct length for each size, add 4 (4, 5, 7) extra single-color rnds at the points marked by an asterisk (*) on the chart = a total of 24 (24, 30, 42) extra rnds. *At the same time*, pm at each side, moving marker up as you work.

Finishing
See also Tips and Tricks on page 130. Weave in all ends neatly on WS. Join 21 (23, 26, 29) sts with Kitchener st for each shoulder. Place the remaining 88 (92) sts for the neck on smaller circular.

Neckband
Pm for beg of rnd. Purl 1 rnd and then work 6 rnds stockinette, increasing 2 sts at each side = 4 sts over the rnd on every rnd. BO loosely (= facing). Fold the facing to the wrong side and sew down loosely.

Attach Sleeves
Measure the width at the top of the sleeve and then measure half the total sleeve top width down each side for the armhole. Baste line for armhole.

Machine-stitch a double row of zigzag stitching on each side of the marking thread. Carefully cut open each armhole between the lines of stitching. With WS of sleeve facing on WS of body, attach sleeves with fine back stitching. Fold facing over the cut edges and sew down loosely.

Blocking
Dampen the sweater in lukewarm water. Gently squeeze out the water. Place a large towel on the floor and put sweater on top. Roll up the towel and press out excess water. Lay the sweater flat on a dry towel or on a sweater drying rack and leave until completely dry.

KARPE DIEM SWEATER FOR CHILDREN—ROUND YOKE

Sizes (years)	2	4	6
Chest	25½ in / 65 cm	28 in / 71 cm	29½ in / 75 cm
Total Length	14½ in / 37 cm	17¼ in / 44 cm	19¾ in / 50 cm
Sleeve Length to Underarm	9¾ in / 24 cm	11 in / 28 cm	12¼ in / 31 cm

Yarn and Yarn Amounts
CYCA #3 (DK/light worsted) Mitu from Rauma (100% wool, 109 yd/100 m / 50 g). You can substitute yarn that knits to a gauge of 22 sts in 4 in / 10 cm.

Color Suggestions	2	(4)	6
SFN 90 Dark Brown	100	100	150 gram
SFN 70 Medium Brown	100	100	150 gram
SFN 73 Beige	50	100	100 gram
0244 Petroleum	50	50	50 gram
5775 Turquoise	50	50	50 gram

Needles
U.S. sizes 2-3 and 4 / 3 and 3.5 mm: short circulars and set of 5 dpn

Gauge
22 sts and 28 rnds *on larger needles* = 4 x 4 in / 10 x 10 cm.
Adjust needle sizes to obtain correct gauge if necessary.

Sleeves
With smaller size dpn and Dark Brown, CO 40 (44, 44) sts. Divide sts onto dpn and join. Work around in k2, p2 ribbing for 12 rnds. Change to larger size dpn and pm at center of underarm. Now work following the charted pattern (see page 25).
Increase 1 st on each side of marker approx. every 4th-5th (5th, 5th) rnd until there are a total of 64 (68, 72) sts.

NOTE: To have the correct length for each size, add 0 (3, 6) extra single-color rnds at the points marked by an asterisk (*) on the chart = a total of 0 (9, 18) extra rnds.

When you reach the point on the chart where the sleeves should be attached, BO 8 sts centered at underarm (= BO 4 sts on each side of marker). Set piece aside and make another sleeve the same way.

Body
The body is worked in the round on a circular ndl. With Dark Brown and smaller circular, CO 144 (156, 164) sts. Join, being careful not to twist cast-on row; pm for beginning of rnd. Work 12 rnds in k2, p2 ribbing.

Change to larger circular and work in pattern following the chart on page 25. *At the same time*, pm at each side, moving markers up as you work.

NOTE: To have the correct length for each size, add 0 (3, 6) extra single-color rnds at the points marked by an asterisk (*) on the chart = a total of 0 (18, 36) extra rnds.

Where indicated on the chart for start of yoke, BO 8 sts centered at each underarm (= BO 4 sts on each side of marker). Place sleeves on circular with body and begin the round yoke.

Yoke
The body and sleeves should now be arranged on circular as: back, sleeve, front, sleeve = a total of 240 (260, 278) sts. Continue following the chart on page 25, decreasing as indicated on the chart. The number of sts to be decreased in each decrease round is shown in the table on page 25. Work all decreases as k2tog.

Round Yoke—Number of Stitches to Decrease

Sizes (years)	2	4	6
Total stitches at beginning of yoke	240	260	278
1st decrease	36 sts, approx. every 6th-7th st	36 sts, approx. every 6th-7th st	40 sts, approx. every 7th st
Sts rem after 1st dec rnd	204	224	238
2nd decrease	40 sts, approx. every 5th st	37 sts, approx. every 6th st	41 sts, approx. every 5th-6th st
Sts rem after 2nd dec rnd	164	187	197
3rd decrease	36 sts, approx. every 4th-5th st	40 sts, approx. every 4th-5th st	40 sts, approx. every 5th st
Sts rem after 3rd dec rnd	128	147	157
4th decrease	32 sts, approx. every 4th st	39 sts, approx. every 3rd-4th st	45 sts, approx. every 3rd-4th st
Sts rem after 4th dec rnd*	96	108	112

*After the 4th decrease rnd, make sure the neck opening will fit the person receiving the sweater.

Neckband

Change to smaller circular and work around in k2, p2 ribbing for 8 rnds. Work 1 rnd of eyelets for foldline = (K2tog, yo) around. Work 8 rnds k2, p2 ribbing and then BO loosely in ribbing.

Finishing

Seam underarms and then weave in all ends neatly on WS.

Blocking

Dampen the sweater in lukewarm water. Gently squeeze out the water. Place a large towel on the floor and put sweater on top. Roll up the towel and press out excess water. Lay the sweater flat on a dry towel or on a sweater drying rack and leave until completely dry.

Children's Round Yoke Sweater—Body and Sleeves

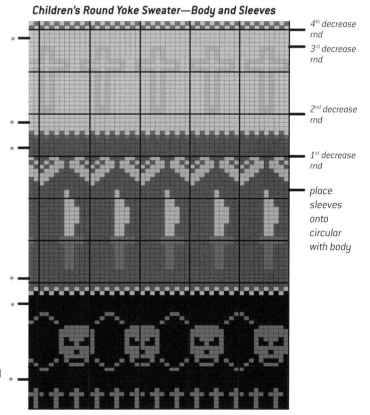

4th decrease rnd

3rd decrease rnd

2nd decrease rnd

1st decrease rnd

place sleeves onto circular with body

*Knit 0 (3, 6) extra single-color rounds here

Animals in Africa

We knitted a sweater in bright, fun colors that children will love. African animals are always popular and children love to dress in brilliant colors that make them happy. Simply said, the combination of colors and animals will put anyone in a good mood. Maybe we adults would be perked up by using more colors?

The sweater is not just fun to look at but also fun to knit. For the most part, it's worked with only two colors per round, but the sections with eyes have three colors. If you think this will be too hard to knit, you can embroider the eyes on later with duplicate stitch.

The lining of the sweater's neckband is orange, a good contrast with turquoise. The neckband is not very high by design, so the orange will show.

JUNGLE SWEATER – T-SHIRT SHAPING

Sizes (years)	1	2	4
Chest	24½ in / 62 cm	26 in / 66 cm	28 in / 71 cm
Total Length	13 in / 33 cm	14½ in / 37 cm	17¼ in / 41 cm
Sleeve Length to Underarm	9 in / 23 cm	10¾ in / 27 cm	11¾ in / 30 cm

Yarn and Yarn Amounts

(CYCA #3) Falk from Dale of Norway (100% wool, 116 yd/106 m / 50 g) or Mitu from Rauma (50% wool, 50% alpaca, 109 yd/100 m / 50 g). You can substitute yarn that knits to a gauge of 22 sts in 4 in / 10 cm.

Color Suggestions		1	2	4
	Falk 9133 Light Green or Mitu 6315 Grass	50	50	50
	Falk 4018 Red or Mitu 4932 Red	50	50	50
	Falk 3072 Chocolate or Mitu SFN 70 Camel	50	50	50
	Falk 8246 Christmas Green or Mitu 5340 Green	50	50	50
	Falk 5646 Bright Blue or Mitu 4922 Royal Blue	50	50	50
	Falk 2427 Yellow or Mitu 6240 Yellow	50	50	50
	Falk 5815 Turquoise or Mitu 5775 Turquoise	100	100	100
	Falk 3309 Marigold or Mitu 0784 Orange	50	50	50

Needles

U.S. sizes 2-3 and 4 / 3 and 3.5 mm: long and short circulars and set of 5 dpn

Gauge

22 sts and 29 rnds on larger needles = 4 x 4 in / 10 x 10 cm.
Adjust needle sizes to obtain correct gauge if necessary.

Please read the introductory sections of this book before you begin knitting.

Sleeves

With smaller size dpn and Bright Blue, CO 40 (42, 44) sts. Divide sts evenly onto dpn and join. Work 8 rnds in stockinette for the facing and then 1 eyelet rnd: (k2tog, yo) around. Change to larger size dpn.

Now work following the charted pattern. Pm at the center of the underarm and move it up as you work. *At the same time* as working the pattern, increase 1 st at each side of the marker approx every 4th-5th rnd until there are a total of 70 (74, 78) sts.

NOTE: Adjust the sleeve length by working more single-color rnds before and after the panels. The chart is written for the smallest size (1 year). For the correct sleeve length, work 0 (1, 2) extra rounds in the main color between each of the panels for a total of 0 (10, 20) extra rnds. Distribute the extra rnds above and below the panels.

When sleeve measures 9 (10¾, 11¾) in / 23 (27, 30) cm or desired length, work facing. Turn the sleeve inside out and knit 6 rnds in stockinette. On each rnd, increase 1 st before and after the center underarm marker. BO loosely. Set piece aside and make another sleeve the same way.

Body

With smaller size circular and Bright Blue, CO 136 (146, 156) sts; join, being careful not to twist cast-on row. Pm for beginning of rnd. Work 8 rnds in stockinette for the facing and then 1 eyelet rnd: (k2tog, yo) around. Change to larger size circular. Now work following the charted pattern. Pm at each side and move up markers as you work.

NOTE: Adjust the body length by working more single-color rnds before and after the panels. The chart is written for the smallest size (1 year). To have the correct length for each size, add 0 (1, 2) extra single-color rnds for a total of 0 (12, 24) extra rnds. Distribute the extra rnds above and below the panels.

When body measures 13 (14½, 17¼) in / 33 (37, 41) cm from foldline, work the last rnd as follows: Work 14 (17, 19) sts, BO 40 (40, 40) sts for front neck, k82 (89, 97).

Finishing
See also Tips and Tricks on page 130.

Weave in all ends neatly on WS. Join 14 (17, 19) sts with Kitchener st for each shoulder. Place back neck stitches on a holder.

Neckband
Baste the front neckline (see sweater photos for shaping) and then work fine zigzag stitching along basting. Cut away extra fabric above machine-stitching. With Turquoise, use tip of smaller size circular or crochet hook to pick up and knit stitches along front neck (just below machine stitching. Place held back neck sts on circular and knit. Pm for beg of rnd and knit 2 rounds. Work an eyelet rnd: (k2tog, yo) around. Change to Marigold for the facing. Knit 4 rnds and then BO loosely. Fold the lining to the WS and sew down to cover cut edges.

Attach Sleeves
Measure the width at the top of the sleeve and then measure half the total sleeve top width down each side for the armhole. Baste line for armhole. Machine-stitch a double row of zigzag stitching on each side of the basting thread. Carefully cut open each armhole centered between the lines of stitching. With WS of sleeve facing on WS of body, attach sleeves with fine

back stitching. Fold facing over the cut edges and sew down loosely.

Fold each sleeve cuff and bottom edge facing along eyelet round to WS and sew down.

Blocking
Dampen the sweater in lukewarm water. Gently squeeze out the water. Place a large towel on the floor and put sweater on top. Roll up the towel and press out excess water. Lay the sweater flat on a dry towel or on a sweater drying rack and leave until completely dry.

Body and Sleeves

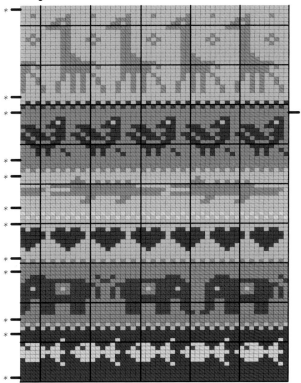

*Add extra rounds for 2- and 4-year sizes

sleeves here

I Know a Lovely Garden

where roses are in bloom. God created it as a gift for all the children of the earth.

When she was little, Cecilie was allowed to choose a good night song every evening before she went to sleep. Her choice was almost always this song. Since then, she has always been taken with gardens and flowers. This sweater is for anyone who likes to relax in a garden. It's knitted in a lovely, fine alpaca yarn that is light and warm.

In the garden at her cottage, Cecilie raises California poppies that shine against the blue water. They were the inspiration for the poppy panels which gave the sweater its spark. Otherwise, we've chosen the flowers we like best. If you have charts for your favorite flower all you have to do is substitute it in one of the panels. One amusing detail is the row of ladybugs around the neckband.

GARDEN SWEATER—ROUND YOKE

Sizes	S	M	L	XL
Chest	35 in / 89 cm	37½ in / 95 cm	40¼ in / 102 cm	43¾ in / 111 cm
Total Length	26½ in / 67 cm	26½ in / 67 cm	27½ in / 70 cm	27½ in / 70 cm
Sleeve Length to Underarm	18¼ in / 46 cm	18½ in / 47 cm	19 in / 48 cm	19 in / 48 cm

Yarn and Yarn Amounts

CYCA #1 (sock/fingering/baby) Tynn Alpakka from Du Store Alpakka (100% alpaca, 183 yd/167 m / 50 g). We also used 1 ball of Inca from Rauma (100% superfine alpaca, 191 yd/175 m / 50 g). If you like, you can use Rauma's Inca for all the colors or substitute yarn that knits to a gauge of 27 sts in 4 in / 10 cm.

Color Suggestions	S	M	L	XL
Tynn Alpakka 186 Seagreen Heather or Inca 588 Country Blue	400	450	500	550 gram
Tynn Alpakka 134 Orange or Inca 250 Orange	50	50	50	50
Tynn Alpakka 164 Green Heather or Inca 743 Olive	100	100	100	100
Tynn Alpakka 157 Yellow or Inca 633 Mustard	50	50	50	50
Tynn Alpakka 150 Raspberry or Inca 109 Cerise	50	50	50	50
Tynn Alpakka 101 Natural White or Inca 010 Natural	50	50	50	50
Tynn Alpakka 109 Black or Inca 050 Black	50	50	50	50
Inca 059 Red	50	50	50	50

Needles

U.S. sizes 1-2 and 2-3 / 2.5 and 3 mm: long and short circulars and set of 5 dpn

Gauge

27 sts and 30 rnds on larger needles =
4 x 4 in / 10 x 10 cm.
Adjust needle sizes to obtain correct gauge if necessary.

Sleeves

With Seagreen Heather and smaller size dpn, CO 56 (56, 60, 64) sts. Divide sts onto dpn and join. Work 20 rnds k2tbl, p2 ribbing.

Change to larger size dpn and work the charted butterfly motif (see page 35). Work the rest of the sleeve in the main color only. Pm at center of underarm and move it up as you work. Increase 1 st on each side of the marker approx. every 5th rnd until there are a total of 102 (108, 114, 118) sts. Continue until the sleeve is 18¼ (18½, 19, 19) in / 46 (47, 48, 48) cm long or desired length.

BO 5 sts on each side of the underarm marker (10 sts total). Set piece aside and make another sleeve the same way.

Body

With Seagreen Heather and smaller circular, CO 240 (256, 276, 300) sts. Join, being careful not to twist cast-on row; pm for beginning of rnd. Work 20 rnds k2tbl, p2 ribbing. Change to larger circular and work the charted pattern on page 35. Pm at each side and move up markers as you work.

NOTE: To have the correct length for each size, for Sizes S and M, work 6 rnds with MC instead of 8 between the panels from the butterflies to the pansies = a total of 10 fewer rounds.

When you've reached the start of the yoke, BO 5 sts at each side of underarm marker, on each side of sweater (= BO 10 sts at each side; 20 sts total).

Yoke

The body and sleeves should now be arranged on

circular as: back, sleeve, front, sleeve = a total of 404 (432, 464, 496) sts. Continue, following the pattern chart and decreasing as indicated on the chart. The number of sts to be decreased in each decrease round is shown in the table below. Work all decreases as k2tog. After the 7th decrease rnd, make sure the neck will fit the wearer.

Round Yoke—Number of Stitches to Decrease

Sizes	S	M	L	XL
Total stitches at beginning of yoke	404	432	464	496
1st decrease	36 sts, approx. every 11th st	45 sts, approx. every 9th-10th st	46 sts, approx. every 10th st	48 sts, approx. every 10th st
Sts rem after 1st dec rnd	368	387	418	448
2nd decrease	36 sts, approx. every 10th st	40 sts, approx. every 9th-10th st	46 sts, approx. every 9th st	50 sts, approx. every 9th st
Sts rem after 2nd dec rnd	332	347	372	398
3rd decrease	32 sts, approx. every 10th st	36 sts, approx. every 9th-10th st	35 sts, approx. every 10th-11th st	40 sts, approx. every 10th st
Sts rem after 3rd dec rnd	300	311	337	358
4th decrease	40 sts, approx. every 7th-8th st	40 sts, approx. every 8th st	45 sts, approx. every 7th-8th st	50 sts, approx. every 7th st
Sts rem after 4th dec rnd	260	271	292	308
5th decrease	40 sts, approx. every 6th-7th st	40 sts, approx. very 7th st	50 sts, approx. every 6th st	55 sts, approx. every 5th-6th st
Sts rem after 5th dec rnd	220	231	242	253
6th decrease	50 sts, approx. every 4th-5th st	55 sts, approx. every 4th st	60 sts, approx. every 4th st	65 sts, approx. every 4th st
Sts rem after 6th dec rnd	170	176	182	188
7th decrease	38 sts, approx. every 4th-5th st	44 sts, approx. every 4th st	46 sts, approx. every 4th st	52 sts, approx. every 3rd-4th st
Sts rem after 7th dec rnd*	132	132	136	136

*After the 7th decrease rnd, make sure the neck will fit the wearer.

Neckband
With larger circular, work the neckband following the chart. After completing ladybug panel, knit 2 rnds with MC and then work 1 rnd of eyelets for foldline = (k2tog, yo) around. Work 12 rnds stockinette and then BO loosely. Fold the facing to WS and sew down.

Finishing
Seam underarms and then weave in all ends neatly on WS.

Blocking
Dampen the sweater in lukewarm water. Gently squeeze out the water. Place a large towel on the floor and put sweater on top. Roll up the towel and press out excess water. Lay the sweater flat on a dry towel or on a sweater drying rack and leave until completely dry.

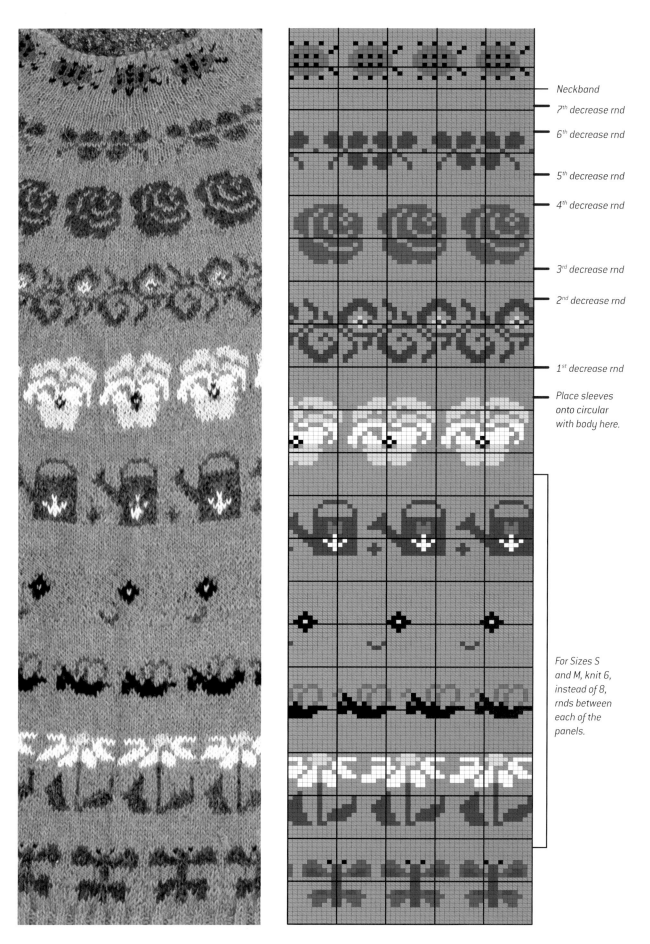

Neckband

7th decrease rnd

6th decrease rnd

5th decrease rnd

4th decrease rnd

3rd decrease rnd

2nd decrease rnd

1st decrease rnd

Place sleeves onto circular with body here.

For Sizes S and M, knit 6, instead of 8, rnds between each of the panels.

Happy Colors for Your Feet

Cozy socks for those cold winter days, when you can happily look forward to spring and the tulips soon to bloom!

This is a typical leftover yarn project. Since many colors are used, it could be expensive if you had to buy all the yarn. If you only have a little of each leftover color, you can, for example, tie all the pinks together for the pink color. That will make the tulips extra pretty! To make a little ball of similar colors, simply tie strands each about 20 in / 50 cm long together and then wind the yarn into a ball. If you aren't practiced at weaving in yarn ends as you knit, weaving in all the ends afterwards will be a little tedious but you'll have so many different color nuances that it's absolutely worth the time.

The motifs won't align as you decrease for the gusset and may look a little "off" at the sides but they will match perfectly once you finish the shaping.

By choice, we decided not to adjust the stitch counts for all the motifs to match up. That's because the main concept of hen knitting is that the knitter should decide what motifs to use. It's much easier to be creative if you don't have to worry about aligning every panel or motif. It's not the end of the world if the motifs are a little skewed along the decrease lines—they are just fun variations!

TULIP SOCKS—INSTRUCTIONS

Sizes: Women's U.S. 8-9 / European 38/40

Yarn and Yarn Amounts

CYCA #2 (sport/baby) PT5 from Rauma (80% wool, 20% nylon, 140 yd/128 m / 50 g)

Color Suggestions		Grams
	548 Pink	50
	515 Yellow	50
	582 Light Green	50
	571 Turquoise	50
	571 Turquoise	50

Needles

U.S. sizes 2-3 and 4 / 3 and 3.5 mm: set of 5 dpn

Gauge

24 sts on larger needles = 4 x 4 in / 10 x 10 cm. Adjust needle sizes to obtain correct gauge if necessary.

Leg

With smaller size dpn and Turquoise, CO 66 sts. Divide sts onto dpn and join, being careful not to twist cast-on row. Work 5 rnds k1, p1 ribbing. Change to larger size dpn and work the charted pattern for the leg.

NOTE: Begin at the top of the chart and work down so the tulips will be facing up on the leg. After completing leg chart, place 33 sts on a holder for the instep. Work the heel (see chart) over the remaining 33 sts until it is 2½ in / 6 cm long.

Heel Turn (continue in heel flap pattern)

Row 1 (RS): Knit across until 9 sts rem, sl 1, k1, psso; turn.
Row 2 (WS): Purl across until 9 sts rem, sl 1, p1, psso; turn.
Row 3: Knit across until 8 sts rem, sl 1, k1, psso; turn.
Row 4: Purl across until 8 sts rem, sl 1, p1, psso; turn.
Continue the same way with 1 less st before the decrease on each pair of RS/WS rows until 17 sts rem.

Foot

With Blue, pick up and knit 12 sts on each side of the heel flap and work the 33 instep sts = 12 + 33 + 12 + 17 = 74 sts. Work the charted foot pattern (don't forget to work from the top down on the chart) and, *at the same time*, on every other rnd, decrease 1 st before/after instep until a total of 8 sts have been

decreased and 66 sts rem. Continue until foot chart is complete and then work the toe (see below).

Toe Shaping

Change to Toe chart and decrease 2 sts at each side of instep and sole as follows:
Begin rnd at instep: Ssk, knit until 2 sts rem on instep, k2tog. Work the same way across the sole. Decrease on the 1st, 5th, 8th, and 10th rnds and then on every rnd until 8 sts rem. K2tog around; cut yarn and draw end through rem sts. Tighten yarn end and weave in all ends neatly on WS.
Make the second sock the same way.

Leg—*begin at the top of the chart and work down*

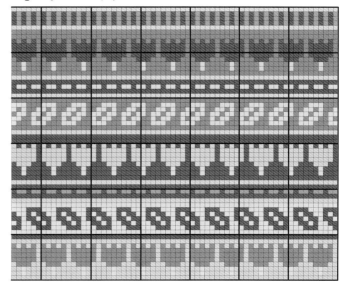

Heel and Toe

Foot—*begin at the top of the chart and work down*

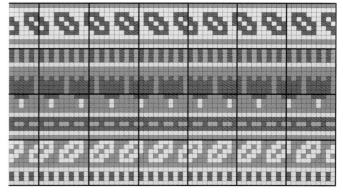

The Mackerels Are In!

Hunting and fishing are important sources of inspiration for us in Norway. There is no better food than something you've caught yourself, whether it's freshly boiled crab or smoked mackerel with herbs fresh from the garden.

This sweater features motifs from the sea. If you look closely, you'll find crabs, manatees, flounder, mackerel, squid, porpoises, and sea trout. Most of these can be found in the waters around Norway, except for the seahorses. The only seahorses we know about in Norway are in the lagoon at the State Oil Office.

Seahorses are usually found in tropical waters; some populations are now threatened by overfishing and destruction of their natural habitat. We have included them on the sweater because we think they are pretty and they remind us that we need to care for nature and be considerate of all creatures—even ones we eat for dinner.

This sweater is designed for anyone who enjoys catching mackerel or flounder. It is always good to have something to keep you warm when out fishing, so this sweater is extra-long. If you want a shorter sweater, simply eliminate one of the panels—but we think it will be hard to decide which one. Great fishing!

SEA SWEATER—ROUND YOKE

Sizes	S	M	L	XL
Chest	36¾ in / 93 cm	39½ in / 100 cm	42¼ in / 107 cm	45¼ in / 115 cm
Total Length	26½ in / 67 cm	27½ in / 70 cm	29¼ in / 74 cm	29¼ in / 74 cm
Sleeve Length to Underarm	18¼ in / 46 cm	19 in / 48 cm	20½ in / 52 cm	20½ in / 52 cm

Yarn and Yarn Amounts

CYCA #3 (DK/light worsted) Smart from Sandnes (100% wool, 108 yd/99 m / 50 g) OR CYCA #3 (DK/light worsted) Mitu from Rauma (50% wool, 50% alpaca, 109 yd/100 m / 50 g). You can substitute yarn that knits to a gauge of 22 sts in 4 in / 10 cm.

Color Suggestions		S	M	L	XL
	Smart 6545 Petroleum or Mitu 0244 Petroleum	500	500	500	500
	Smart 3051 Khaki or Mitu SFN 61 Sand	0	0	100	100
	Smart 9544 Olive or Mitu 5340 Green	100	100	50	50
	Smart 3082 Brown or Mitu SFN 90 Brown	100	100	100	100
	Smart 2527 Ochre or Mitu 7255 Ochre	100	100	100	100
	Smart 6355 Fly Blue* or Mitu 1900 Dark Green	50	50	50	50
	Smart 5904 Medium Blue* or Mitu 7244 Light Blue-green	50	50	50	50
	Smart 1042 Gray Heather or Mitu SFN 41 Gray	100	100	100	100

*The original colors used for the sweater in the photo are no longer available. We used the most similar colors.

Needles

U.S. sizes 2-3 and 4 / 3 mm and 3.5 mm: long and short circulars and set of 5 dpn

Gauge

22 sts and 29 rnds on larger needles =
4 x 4 in / 10 x 10 cm.
Adjust needle sizes to obtain correct gauge
if necessary.

Round Yoke—Number of Stitches to Decrease

Sizes	S	M	L	XL
Total stitches at beginning of yoke	336	360	384	408
1st decrease	30 sts, approx. every 11th st	36 sts, approx. every 10th st	42 sts, approx. every 9th st	39 sts, approx. every 10th-11th st
Sts rem after 1st dec rnd	306	324	342	369
2nd decrease	36 sts, approx. every 8th-9th st	36 sts, approx. every 9th st	36 sts, approx. every 9th-10th st	45 sts, approx. every 8th st
Sts rem after 2nd dec rnd	270	288	306	324
3rd decrease	36 sts, approx. every 7th-8th st	36 sts, approx. every 8th st	36 sts, approx. every 8th-9th st	36 sts, approx. every 9th st
Sts rem after 3rd dec rnd	234	252	270	288
4th decrease	26 sts, approx. every 9th st	28 sts, approx. every 9th st	30 sts, approx. every 9th st	32 sts, approx. every 9th st
Sts rem after 4th dec rnd	208	224	240	256
5th decrease	46 sts, approx. every 4th-5th st	53 sts, approx. every 4th st	60 sts, approx. every 4th st	58 sts, approx. every 4th st
Sts rem after 5th dec rnd	162	171	180	198
6th decrease	22 sts, approx. every 7th st	23 sts, approx every 7th st	24 sts, approx. every 7th-8th st	30 sts, approx. every 6th-7th st
Sts rem after 6th dec rnd	140	148	156	168
Sts rem after 6th dec rnd	20 sts, approx. every 7th st	24 sts, approx. every 6th st	28 sts, approx. every 5th-6th st	34 sts, approx. every 5th st
Sts rem after 7th dec rnd*	120	124	128	134

*After the 7th decrease rnd, make sure the neck will fit the wearer.

Sleeves

With Petroleum and smaller size dpn, CO 46 (48, 50, 52) sts. Divide sts onto dpn and join. Work 16 (22, 22, 22) rnds k1tbl, p1 ribbing.

Change to larger size dpn and work the charted motifs as follows:
Sizes S and M: Work Chart B before you begin Chart A at the marker for your size.
Sizes L and XL: Work Chart A immediately following the ribbing.

Pm at center of underarm and move it up as you work. Increase 1 st on each side of the marker approx. every 6th rnd until there are a total of 86 (90, 94, 98) sts. Work to point on chart indicating the row for joining the sleeves and body. BO 5 sts on each side of the underarm marker (10 sts total). Set piece aside and make another sleeve the same way.

Body

With Petroleum and smaller circular, CO 204 (220, 236, 252) sts. Join, being careful not to twist cast-on row; pm for beginning of rnd. Work 16 (22, 22, 22) rnds k1tbl, p1 ribbing.
Change to larger circular and work the charted motifs as follows:
Sizes S and M: Work Chart B before you begin Chart

A at the marker for your size.

Sizes L and XL: Work Chart A immediately following the ribbing.

Pm at each side and move up markers as you work.

When you've reached the start of the yoke, BO 5 sts at each side of underarm marker, on each side of sweater (= BO 10 sts at each side; 20 sts total).

Yoke
The body and sleeves should now be arranged on circular as: back, sleeve, front, sleeve = a total of 336 (360, 384, 408) sts. Continue following the pattern chart, decreasing as indicated on the chart. The number of sts to be decreased in each decrease round is shown in the table. Work all decreases as k2tog. After the 7th decrease rnd, make sure the neck will fit the wearer.

TIPS
Some of the decreases fall in the center of a pattern. Try to adjust the decreases so that the motif isn't distorted too much, but don't be afraid of small changes either. These little adjustments will make the sweater completely unique.

Neckband
With Petroleum and smaller circular, work 8 rnds of k1tbl, p1 ribbing (approx. 1¼ in / 3 cm). Work 1 rnd of eyelets for foldline = (k2tog, yo) around. Work 10 rnds k1tbl, p1 ribbing and then BO loosely in ribbing. Fold the facing to WS and sew down.

Finishing
Seam underarms and then weave in all ends neatly on WS.

Blocking
Dampen the sweater in lukewarm water. Gently squeeze out the water. Place a large towel on the floor and put sweater on top. Roll up the towel and press out excess water. Lay the sweater flat on a dry towel or on a sweater drying rack and leave until completely dry.

Chart B

Chart A

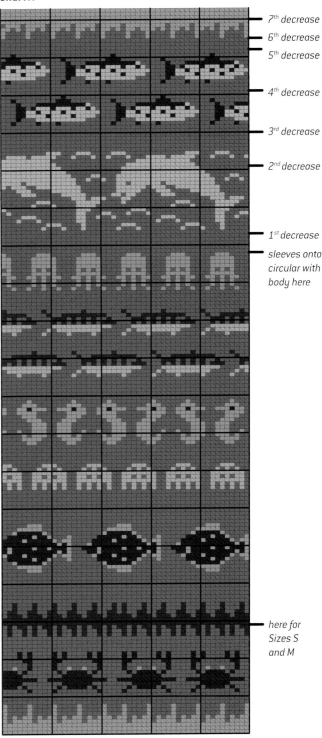

7th decrease
6th decrease
5th decrease
4th decrease
3rd decrease
2nd decrease
1st decrease
sleeves onto circular with body here

here for Sizes S and M

Little Sailor

When out on the lake, little sailors need a warm and soft sweater and this one is extra cozy with its motifs from the coast: ducks, fish, hearts, fishing boats, gulls, and sail boats. We've also added a panel for the little one's name.

We've chosen blue and brown tones but, of course, you can use a different color scheme. This sweater is perfect for leftover yarns. If you have to buy the yarn, you'll end up with some leftovers, but you can easily use them for another sweater, or maybe a little hat.

The sweater has a round neck extending to a buttoned shoulder band so you can easily slip it on over the head.

MARITIME BABY SWEATER—T-SHIRT SHAPING

Sizes (months)	6	9	12
Chest	22 in / 56 cm	23 ¼ in / 59 cm	24 ¾ in / 63 cm
Total Length	13 in / 33 cm	14 ½ in / 37 cm	15 in / 38 cm
Sleeve Length to Underarm	7 ½ in / 19 cm	8 ¾ in / 22 cm	9 ½ in / 24 cm

Yarn and Yarn Amounts

CYCA #1 (sock/fingering/baby) Baby Ull from Viking of Norway (100% Merino wool, 191 yd/175 m / 50 g).
and CYCA #1 (sock/fingering/baby) Baby Ull from Gjestal (100% Merino wool, 191 yd/175 m / 50 g).

You can substitute yarn that knits to a gauge of 27 sts in 4 in / 10 cm.

Notions
2 small buttons

Color Suggestions		6	9	12
	Viking Baby Ull 307 Beige	50	50	50
	Gjestal Baby Ull 856 Brown	50	50	50
	Gjestal Baby Ull 800 Natural White	50	50	50
	Viking Baby Ull 323 Light Turqoise*	50	50	50
	Viking Baby Ull 329 Dark Turquoise	50	50	50
	Gjestal Baby Ull 824 Sky Blue	50	50	50

*The color in the model shown here was a leftover yarn; the color listed in the table is the most similar.

Needles

U.S. sizes 1-2 and 2-3 / 2.5 and 3 mm: short circulars and set of 5 dpn

Gauge

27 sts and 30 rnds on larger needles = 4 x 4 in / 10 x 10 cm.
Adjust needle sizes to obtain correct gauge if necessary.

Sleeves

With smaller size dpn and Beige, CO 40 (44, 44) sts. Divide sts onto dpn and join. Work around in k1, p1 ribbing for 8 (12, 12) rnds. Change to larger size dpn and knit 1 rnd, increasing 6 sts evenly spaced around to 46 (50, 50) sts.

Now work following the charted pattern for the sleeves. Pm at the center of the underarm and move marker up as you work. *At the same time as working the pattern, increase 1 st at each side of the marker approx. every 5th (5th, 5th) rnd until there are a total of 64 (70, 74) sts.*

NOTE: Stop where indicated on the chart for 6-month size. Work the complete chart for the 9-month size. For the 12-month size, after completing charted rows, work another 7 rnds of the top panel.

When sleeve is 7½ (8¾, 9½) in / 19 (22, 24) cm long, turn the sleeve inside out and knit 6 rnds in stockinette for the facing. On each rnd, increase 1 st before and after the center marker. BO loosely. Set piece aside and make another sleeve the same way.

Body

With smaller circular and Beige, CO 150 (160, 170) sts; join, being careful not to twist cast-on row. Pm for beginning of rnd. Work around in k1, p1 ribbing for 8 (12, 12) rnds. Change to larger circular and work following the charted pattern for the body.

NOTE: Stop where indicated on the chart for 6-month size. Work the complete chart for the 9-month size. For the 12-month size, after completing charted rows, work another 4 rnds of the top panel.

Sleeve Chart

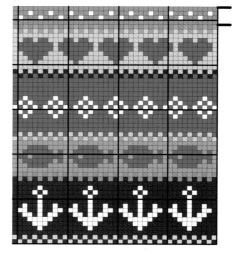

Work another 7 rnds of top motif for 12-month size

End here for 6-month size

Body Chart

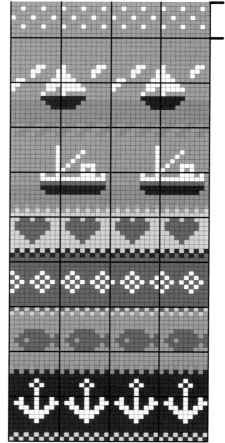

Work another 4 rnds of top motif for 12-month size

End here for 6-month size

49

At the same time, pm at each side, moving marker up as you work.

When the body measures 13 (14½, 15) in / 33 (37, 38) cm, work the last rnd as follows: K18 (20, 21) sts, BO 40 (40, 44) sts for front neck, k92 (100, 105) sts.

Finishing
See also Tips and Tricks on page 130.

Seam the right shoulder with 18 (20, 21) sts in Kitchener st. Seam the first 4 (4, 5) sts from armhole for left shoulder. Transfer rest of sts to smaller circular.

Neckband and Left Shoulder Bands
Baste the front neckline (see sweater photos for shaping) and then work fine zigzag stitching at basting. Cut away extra fabric around neckline. Use a crochet hook to pick up stitches with Sky Blue along the neckline (just below machine stitching) and work band back and forth on smaller circular. Beginning at front left shoulder, work 4 rows k1, p1 ribbing across left shoulder and around neck.
On the next row, make two buttonholes on back left shoulder: Work until 14 (16, 16) sts rem. Rib 4 sts, yo, k2tog, work 2 (4, 4) sts in ribbing, yo, k2tog, work last 4 sts in ribbing. Now work 3 more rows k1, p1 ribbing.

On the next row, BO for left shoulder: BO 14 (16, 16) sts on left front shoulder, finish row in ribbing. Next row: BO 14 (16, 16) sts on back left shoulder, complete row.

Now work the neckband facing over rem sts. Work 8 rows back and forth in k1, p1 ribbing. BO loosely in ribbing. Fold neckband to WS and sew down with overcast stitch over the cut edges and around inside of neck. Sew on 2 buttons spaced as for buttonholes. Sew the outer edge of the shoulder facing on the left shoulder smoothly to the shoulder.

Attach Sleeves
Measure the width at the top of the sleeve and then measure half the total sleeve top width down each side for the armhole. Baste line for armhole. Machine-stitch a double row of zigzag stitching on each side of the basting line. Carefully cut open each armhole between the lines of stitching. Turn sweater body inside out and attach sleeve on WS with fine back stitching. Fold facing over the cut edges and sew down securely.

Blocking
Dampen the sweater in lukewarm water. Gently squeeze out the water. Place a large towel on the floor and put sweater on top. Roll up the towel and press out excess water. Lay the sweater flat on a dry towel or on a sweater drying rack and leave until completely dry.

Ship Ahoy!

We wanted to make some pillows for the house and the cottages by the sea. Shells and crabs, anchors, sail boats, and waves are all motifs you'll find near the sea. We discovered that the pillows fit well in the rocking chair where one can sit and philosophize as dusk falls.

One pillow is two-colored in blue and white while the other has some added details in red. Cecilie picked the colors for one pillow so it would match the sofa at the cabin. There are so many wonderful colors to choose from—use the colors that match the interior where you'll use the pillows.

A knitted pillow cover is stretchy and should be made a little smaller than the pillow form so it won't be too loose.

MARITIME PILLOW COVER WITH ANCHORS

Begin working this pillow with the center front knitted around on a circular. When that is complete, cut it open before adding the edging. When you cut the cover, keep the live sts at the top on the circular so you only have to pick up and knit sts along 3 sides. It will seem a little troublesome in the instructions but it's easier in practice.

After cutting the cover open, the front edging is worked in the round and then the back is worked as an extension of one side of the front. The back is worked back and forth in a single color.

Finished Measurements
19¾ x 19¾ in / 50 x 50 cm

Yarn and Yarn Amounts
CYCA #3 (DK/light worsted) Lerke from Dale of Norway (52% Merino wool, 48% cotton, 125 yd/114 m / 50 g)
OR
CYCA #3 (DK/light worsted) Petunia from Rauma (Per Tryving) (100% cotton, 120 yd/110 m / 50 g)
You can substitute yarn that knits to a gauge of 22 sts in 4 in / 10 cm.

Color Suggestions		Grams
	Lerke 5845 Blue* or Petunia 275 Jeans	350
	Lerke 4236 Robin Red or Petunia 256 Red	50
	Lerke 0020 Natural White or Petunia 221 Cream	200

*The original blue-green used for the pillow shown is no longer available.

Needles
U.S. size 4 / 3.5 mm: short and long circulars

Crochet Hook
U.S. size E-4 / 3.5 mm

Notions
Blunt tapestry needle, pillow form 19¾ x 19¾ in / 50 x 50 cm

Gauge
22 sts and 26 rnds = 4 x 4 in / 10 x 10 cm.
Adjust needle size to obtain correct gauge if necessary.

Front and Back
NOTE: Before you start knitting, read through the instructions completely. The center front is worked first, without the frame around it.

With short circular and Blue, CO 94 sts; join, being careful not to twist cast-on row. Work following the chart, and note that the first st of every round is p1. After completing charted rows, the piece should measure approx. 16½ x 16½ in / 42 x 42 cm.

The frame is worked next but first you have to cut the piece down the purl line at beginning of rnd. On the last rnd, prepare for the cutting by binding off 5 sts centered at the cutting line: BO 2 sts before the purl line, BO the purl st, BO 2 sts after purl st. Machine-stitch a double rows of fine zigzag on each side of the purls. Carefully cut open between the machine stitching. The 89 live sts at top of piece should remain on the circular.

Working the frame in the round
Change to the long circular and pick up and knit sts along the 3 sides without live sts using the crochet hook and Blue. With all of the sts (picked-up and live) on the circular, pm at the center st of each corner. With Blue, work around in stockinette, increasing at each corner on every round: M1 before the corner marker, k the corner st, M1. Work 10 rnds and then BO the sts around the 3 sides with picked-up sts.

Back
Work back and forth in stockinette over the rem 109 sts for the back. When back measures 19¾ in / 50 cm, BO loosely.

Finishing
Weave in all ends neatly on WS. Fold the pieces with WS facing WS and sew together with small back stitching; leaving an opening for the pillow form at center bottom. After blocking (see below), turn the pillow cover right side out and insert the pillow form. With the main color and overcast st, seam the opening.

Blocking
With RS facing out, dampen the pillow cover in lukewarm water. Gently squeeze out the water. Place a large towel on the floor and put pillow cover on top. Roll up the towel and press out excess water. Lay the cover flat on a dry towel or on a sweater drying rack and leave until completely dry.

Maritime Pillow Cover with Anchors

⊡ = purl 1

MARITIME PILLOW COVER WITH ANCHORS

The front and back are each worked separately on a circular needle. Finish by cutting the pieces open and seaming.

Finished Measurements

19¾ x 27½ in / 50 x 70 cm; the pillow cover is approx. 27¼ x 19¼ in / 69 x 49 cm. The cover is stretchy and needs to be smaller than the form to fit well.

Yarn and Yarn Amounts

CYCA #3 (DK/light worsted) Lerke from Dale of Norway (52% Merino wool, 48% cotton, 125 yd/114 m / 50 g
OR
CYCA #3 (DK/light worsted) Petunia from Rauma (Per Tryving) (100% cotton, 120 yd/110 m / 50 g) You can substitute yarn that knits to a gauge of 22 sts in 4 in / 10 cm.

Color Suggestions	Grams
Lerke 5845 Blue* or Petunia 275 Jeans	350
Lerke 0020 Natural White or Petunia 221 Cream	250

*The original blue-green used for the pillow shown is no longer available.

Needles

U.S. size 4 / 3.5 mm: short circular

Crochet Hook

U.S. size E-4 / 3.5 mm

Notions

Blunt tapestry needle, pillow form 19¾ x 27½ in / 50 x 70 cm

Gauge

22 sts and 26 rnds = 4 x 4 in / 10 x 10 cm.
Adjust needle size to obtain correct gauge if necessary.

Front

With circular and Blue, CO 130 sts; join, being careful not to twist cast-on row. Work following the chart, and note that the first st of every round is p1. After completing charted rows, the piece should measure approx. 19¾ in / 50 cm. BO loosely. Machine-stitch a double row of fine zigzag on each side of the purl line and cut open between the stitch lines.

Back

With Blue, CO 180 sts. Knit around with only Blue throughout, always purling the first st of the round. When piece measures approx. 19¾ in / 50 cm, BO loosely. Machine-stitch a double row of fine zigzag on each side of the purl line and cut open between the stitch lines.

Finishing

Weave in all ends neatly on WS. Fold the pieces with WS facing WS and seam the sides (cut edges) with small backstitch. The back will be about 2 in / 5 cm in from the front of the pillow cover at each side (see picture). Seam the top and bottom, leaving an opening for the pillow form at center bottom. Before finishing the pillow, block the cover (see below).

Blocking

With RS facing out, dampen the pillow cover in lukewarm water. Gently squeeze out the water. Place a large towel on the floor and put pillow cover on top. Roll up the towel and press out excess water. Lay the cover flat on a dry towel or on a sweater drying rack and leave until completely dry.

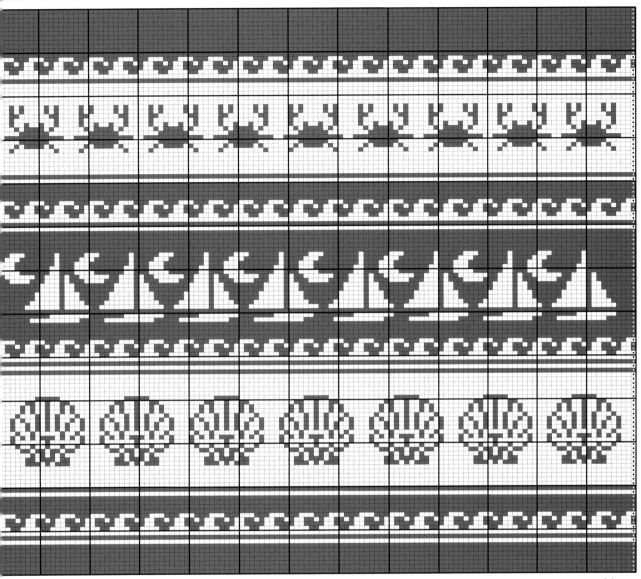

. = purl 1

Twisted Edging

While the pillow dries, make the twisted edging. Cut 8 lengths of Natural White, approx. 6½ yd / 6 meters long (the circumference of the pillow x 2 + a little extra). Knot the strands together at each end and attach one end to a door handle or a similar hook. Begin twisting the strand from the other end. When the strands feel tightly twisted, grab the center and fold the in edging half. Let the ends twist together.

Even out the cord with your fingers and tie a knot at each end.

Finishing Continued

Insert the form into the cover and close the opening with diagonal stitches, leaving a small opening for the twisted cord at center bottom. With white yarn and blunt tapestry needle, sew the cord all around the edge using small overcast sts.

Horses Are Best—No Doubt About It!

Horse riding is a very popular hobby for many. We think that the yarn color for the sweater should match that of the wearer's horse. Just make sure that the main color contrasts well with the pattern colors. We also think the sweater will be well-received if you knit in the name of the stable, horse, or owner on the sweater. See the alphabet and how to center names in the chapter "A Personal Sweater." If you don't want to knit in a name, just work the hearts in the panel.

This sweater has rather large pattern motifs and it pays to be precise when placing the motifs on the sweater. We designed the pattern so that Sizes S and M have 5 horses while Sizes L and XL have 6 horses. To size the sweater correctly, we increased the space between the horses for Sizes M and XL, so the repeats on these sizes will be bigger.

To space the horses symmetrically, it is important that you begin as indicated on the chart. Make sure you follow the correct chart for your size.

HORSE SWEATER—T-SHIRT SHAPING

Sizes	S	M	L	XL
Chest	35 in / 89 cm	38½ in / 98 cm	41¾ in / 106 cm	46 in / 117 cm
Total Length	25¼ in / 64 cm	26½ in / 67 cm	28¼ in / 72 cm	29¼ in / 74 cm
Sleeve Length to Underarm	17¾ in / 45 cm	18¼ in / 46 cm	18½ in / 47 cm	19¼ in / 49 cm

Yarn and Yarn Amounts
CYCA #3 (DK/light worsted) Sterk from Du Store Alpakka (40% Merino wool, 40% alpaca, 20% polyamide, 150 yd/137 m / 50 g). You can substitute yarn that knits to a gauge of 22 sts in 4 in / 10 cm.

Color Suggestions		S	M	L	XL
	822 Gray (MC)	450	450	450	500
	809 Black	150	150	150	150
	813 Petroleum	50	50	50	50

Needles
U.S. sizes 2-3 and 4 / 3 and 3.5 mm: long and short circulars and set of 5 dpn

Gauge
22 sts and 27 rnds on larger needles = 4 x 4 in / 10 x 10 cm.
Adjust needle sizes to obtain correct gauge if necessary.

Sleeves
With Black and smaller size dpn, CO 46 (48, 50, 52) sts. Divide sts onto dpn and join. Knit 8 rnds in stockinette. Make an eyelet rnd for the foldline: (K2tog, yo) around.

Change to larger size dpn and begin the first panel on the chart. Pm at center of underarm and move it up as you work. Increase 1 st on each side of the marker approx. every 5th rnd until there are a total of 90 (94, 98, 102) sts. *At the same time*, after completing horseshoe and heart panel, continue with MC only until the sleeve is 17¾ (18¼, 19, 19¼) in / 45 (46, 47, 49) cm long or desired length.
Turn sleeve inside out and work 6 rnds in stockinette, increasing 1 st on each side of marker at center underarm on every rnd. BO loosely (= facing).

Set piece aside and make another sleeve the same way.

Body
The body is worked in the round on a circular. With Black and smaller circular, CO 195 (215, 234, 258) sts. Join, being careful not to twist cast-on row; pm for beginning of rnd. Knit 8 rnds in stockinette. Make an eyelet rnd for the foldline: (K2tog, yo) around.

Change to larger circular and work the charted pattern. Pm at each side and move up markers as you work. The rnd begins and ends at the left side. Make sure you begin at the marker for your size. This is particularly important for the placement of the horses. After working the heart and horseshoe panel, work in MC for 9 (10¼, 12¼, 13) in / 23 (26, 31, 33) cm before working next motif.

Follow the chart to the last rnd of the neckband. On the last rnd, k25 (29, 34, 35), BO 48 (50, 50, 60) sts for front neck, k rem 122 (136, 150, 163) sts. Seam 25 (29, 34, 35) sts on each shoulder using Kitchener st.

Before finishing the neckband, attach sleeves.

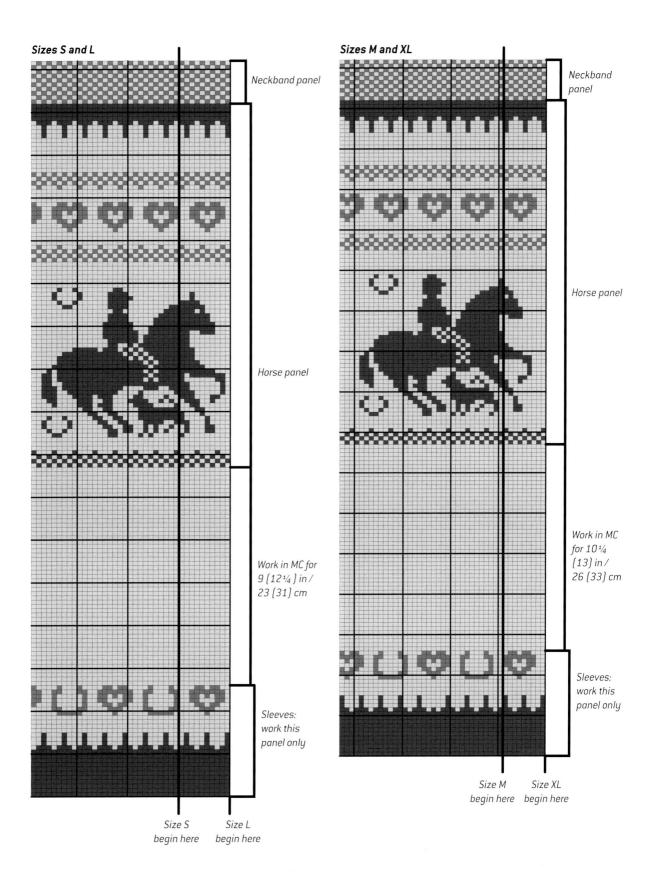

Sizes S and L

Neckband panel

Horse panel

Work in MC for
9 (12¼) in /
23 (31) cm

Sleeves:
work this
panel only

Size S
begin here

Size L
begin here

Sizes M and XL

Neckband
panel

Horse panel

Work in MC
for 10¼
(13) in /
26 (33) cm

Sleeves:
work this
panel only

Size M
begin here

Size XL
begin here

Finishing
See also Tips and Tricks on page 130.

Attaching Sleeves
Measure the width at the top of the sleeve and then measure half the total sleeve top width down each side for the armhole. Baste line for armhole. Machine-stitch a double row of zigzag stitching on each side of the marking thread. Carefully cut open each armhole between the lines of stitching. With WS of facing on WS of sleeve, attach sleeves with fine back stitching. Fold facing over the cut edges and sew down securely. Fold each sleeve cuff and bottom edge facing along eyelet round and sew facings to WS.

Neckband
Baste the front neckline (see sweater photos for shaping) and then work fine zigzag stitching just below basting. Cut away extra fabric above machine stitching. With MC and tip of smaller size circular or crochet hook, pick up and knit stitches along front neck (just below machine stitching). Place held back neck sts onto circular and knit. Pm for beg of rnd and work 12 rnds in charted neckband pattern. Make one rnd of eyelets: (K2tog, yo) around. Work 13 rnds in stockinette with Petroleum and then BO loosely. Fold neckband at eyelet round and sew down loosely on WS, covering cut edges.

Blocking
Dampen the sweater in lukewarm water. Gently squeeze out the water. Place a large towel on the floor and put sweater on top. Roll up the towel and press out excess water. Lay the sweater flat on a dry towel or on a sweater drying rack and leave until completely dry.

Icelandic Ponies

There are about 6,000 Icelandic ponies in Norway and they are the fastest growing horse breed in this country. Many people have fallen for these tough little ponies with their flying manes and tails and sweet temperament. Icelandic ponies are one of the few horses that amble, a four beat lateral gait that should be done with a high knee lift. Riders compete in these gaits and ambling is one of these.

This sweater was inspired by traditional Icelandic sweaters with their round yokes. Of course, traditional Icelandic sweaters usually feature sawtooth motifs and not horses. But there's no reason not to knit an Icelandic pony on a sweater, so we designed one with horses ambling all around the yoke. We also think it would be very well received if you knit in the name of the stable, horse, or owner on the sweater. See "A Personal Sweater" for help knitting and placing the words. If you don't want a name on the sweater, then you can simply knit hearts all the way around in that row.

HORSE SWEATER—ROUND YOKE

Sizes	M/L
Chest	39½ in / 100 cm
Total Length	26¾ in / 68 cm
Sleeve Length to Underarm	19¾ in / 50 cm

Yarn and Yarn Amounts
CYCA #3 (DK/light worsted) Sterk from Du Store Alpakka (40% Merino wool, 40% alpaca, 20% polyamide, 150 yd/137 m / 50 g). You can substitute yarn that knits to a gauge of 22 sts in 4 in / 10 cm.

Color Suggestions		M/L
	806 Natural (MC)	450
	824 Medium Brown	150
	812 Green	50

Needles
U.S. sizes 2-3 and 4 / 3 and 3.5 mm: long and short circulars and set of 5 dpn

Gauge
22 sts and 27 rnds on larger needles = 4 x 4 in / 10 x 10 cm.
Adjust needle sizes to obtain correct gauge if necessary.

TIPS
Knit the name of the horse, stable, or owner in the heart panel.

Sleeves
With Medium Brown and smaller size dpn, CO 50 sts. Divide sts onto dpn and join. Knit 8 rnds in stockinette. Purl 1 rnd for the foldline.

Change to larger size dpn and begin working Chart A. Pm at center of underarm and move it up as you work. Increase 1 st on each side of the marker approx. every 6th rnd until there are a total of 90 sts. After completing heart and horseshoe panel, continue with MC only until the sleeve is 19 in / 48.5 cm long or desired length from the foldline. Work the top panel of Chart A. On the last rnd, BO 5 sts on each side of center underarm marker (= 10 sts bound off). Set sleeve aside and make another sleeve the same way.

Body
The body is worked in the round on a circular. With Medium Brown and smaller circular, CO 220 sts. Join, being careful not to twist cast-on row; pm for beginning of rnd. Knit 8 rnds in stockinette. Purl 1 rnd for the foldline.

Change to larger circular and begin working Chart A. Pm at each side and move up markers as you work. After working the heart and horseshoe panel, work in MC for 17 in / 43 cm (or desired length) from the foldline. Now work the top panel of Chart A.

When you've reached the start of the yoke, BO 5 sts at each side of underarm marker, on each side of sweater (= BO 10 sts at each side; 20 sts total).

Chart A

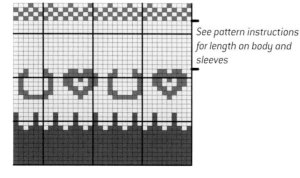

See pattern instructions for length on body and sleeves

Chart B

Yoke

The body and sleeves should now be arranged on circular as: back, sleeve, front, sleeve = a total of 360 sts. Continue, following Charts B and C, decreasing as indicated on the charts. After completing the horses on Chart B, 252 sts remain. The remaining decreases are outlined on the table below. Work all decreases as k2tog. After the 4th decrease rnd, make sure the neck will fit the wearer.

Round Yoke—Number of Stitches to Decrease

Size	M/L
Total sts when sleeves and body are joined	360
Decreases Chart B, Icelandic ponies	108 sts
Sts remaining after decreases	252 sts
1st decrease, Chart C	28 sts, approx. every 9th st
Sts remaining after decreases	224
2nd decrease, Chart C	53 sts, approx. every 4th st
Sts remaining after decreases	171
3rd decrease, Chart C	23 sts, approx. every 7th st
Sts remaining after decreases	148
4th decrease*, Chart C	24 sts, approx. every 6th st
Sts remaining after decreases	124

* Make sure that the neck will fit when making the 4th round of decreases.

Chart C

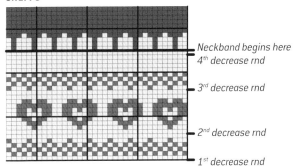

Neckband begins here
4th decrease rnd

3rd decrease rnd

2nd decrease rnd

1st decrease rnd

Neckband

With larger circular, knit the neckband following Chart C. After completing the pattern panel, purl 1 rnd. Knit 8 rnds and then BO loosely. Fold neckband at purl rnd (foldline) and sew down loosely on WS with diagonal stitches.

Finishing

Seam underarms. Fold in facings on body and sleeves and sew down loosely on WS. Weave in all ends neatly on WS.

Blocking

Dampen the sweater in lukewarm water. Gently squeeze out the water. Place a large towel on the floor and put sweater on top. Roll up the towel and press out excess water. Lay the sweater flat on a dry towel or on a sweater drying rack and leave until completely dry.

Ready for the Hunt

You'll need a good warm sweater on fall walks in the mountains when you are looking for birds or berries.

The model shown here is rather simple—just little dog bones at the bottom and the dog motifs at the top. When you are knitting the dog panels, we recommend that you use a place marker (long sticky note, for example) so that you can easily keep your place in the pattern.

There are five dogs on the body of Size M, which means two and a half dogs each on front and back. If you want to center the middle one, we have indicated where to begin on the chart. The 12-year size has four dogs and XL has six so no problems there.

We chose a lovely easy-to-knit alpaca yarn from Du Store Alpakka for this sweater.

DOG SWEATER – SHIRT SHAPING

Sizes	12 years	M	XL
Chest	30¾ in / 78 cm	38½ in / 98 cm	46 in / 117 cm
Total Length	22¾ in / 58 cm	26½ in / 67 cm	29¼ in / 74 cm
Sleeve Length to Underarm	16¼ in / 41 cm	18¼ in / 46 cm	19¼ in / 49 cm

Yarn and Yarn Amounts

CYCA #3 (DK/light worsted) Sterk from Du Store Alpakka (40% Merino wool, 40% alpaca, 20% polyamide, 150 yd/137 m / 50 g). You can substitute yarn that knits to a gauge of 22 sts in 4 in / 10 cm.

Color Suggestions		12 years	M	XL
	824 Medium Brown (MC)	400	550	600
	806 Natural	50	50	50
	A small amount of Black to embroider the dogs' noses and eyes and the bird beaks.			

Needles

U.S. sizes 2-3 and 4 / 3 and 3.5 mm: long and short circulars and set of 5 dpn

Gauge

22 sts and 27 rnds on larger needles = 4 x 4 in / 10 x 10 cm.
Adjust needle sizes to obtain correct gauge if necessary.

Sleeves

With Medium Brown and smaller dpn, CO 48 (50, 52) sts. Divide sts onto dpn and join. Knit 8 rnds in stockinette. Make an eyelet rnd for the foldline: (K2tog, yo) around.

Change to larger dpn and begin the first panel on the chart. Pm at center of underarm and move it up as you work. Increase 1 st on each side of the marker approx. every 5th rnd until there are a total of 82 (94, 102) sts. After completing first panel, continue with MC only until the sleeve is 13 (15, 16¼) in / 33 (38, 41) cm long. Work the panels for the top of the sleeve. Next, turn sleeve inside out and work 6 rnds in stockinette, increasing 1 st on each side of marker at center underarm on every rnd. BO loosely (= facing). Set piece aside and make another sleeve the same way.

Body

The body is worked in the round on a circular. With Medium Brown and smaller circular, CO 172 (215, 258) sts. Join, being careful not to twist cast-on row; pm for beginning of rnd. Knit 8 rnds in stockinette. Make an eyelet rnd for the foldline: (K2tog, yo) around.

Change to larger circular and work the charted pattern. Pm at each side and move up markers as you work. The rnd begins and ends at the left side. Make sure you begin at the marker for your size. After working the bottom panels, work in MC only for 13 ¾ (17 ¼, 20) in / 35 (44, 51) cm before working next motif. Follow the chart to the last rnd of the neckband.

On the last rnd, k21 (29, 35), BO 45 (50, 60) sts for front neck, k rem 106 (136, 163) sts. Seam 21 (29, 35) sts on each shoulder using Kitchener st.

Before finishing the neckband, attach sleeves.

Finishing
See also Tips and Tricks on page 130.

Attaching Sleeves
Measure the width at the top of the sleeve and then measure half the total sleeve top width down each side for the armhole. Baste line for armhole. Machine-stitch a double row of zigzag stitching on each side of the marking thread. Carefully cut open each armhole between the lines of stitching. Turn sweater body inside out and attach sleeves from WS with fine back stitching. Fold facing over the cut edges and sew down securely. Fold each sleeve cuff and bottom edge facing along eyelet round and sew facings to WS.

Neckband
Baste the front neckline (see sweater photos for shaping) and then work fine zigzag stitching just below basting. Cut away extra fabric above machine stitching. With Natural and tip of smaller size circular or crochet hook, pick up and knit stitches along the neckline (just below machine stitching). Place held sts on needle and knit. Pm for beg of rnd and knit 6 rnds. Make one rnd of eyelets: (K2tog, yo) around. Work 7 rnds in stockinette with Natural and

Body

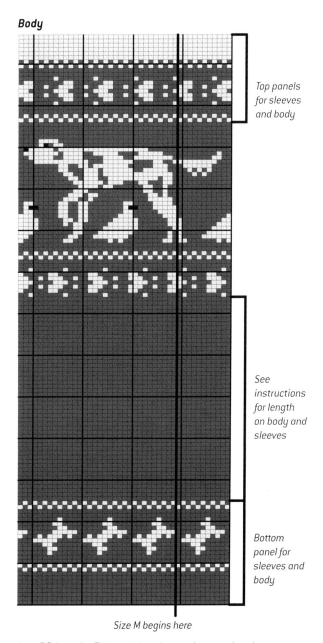

Top panels for sleeves and body

See instructions for length on body and sleeves

Bottom panel for sleeves and body

Size M begins here

then BO loosely. Fold neckband at eyelet round and sew down loosely on WS, covering cut edges.

Blocking
Dampen the sweater in lukewarm water. Gently squeeze out the water. Place a large towel on the floor and put sweater on top. Roll up the towel and press out excess water. Lay the sweater flat on a dry towel or on a sweater drying rack and leave until completely dry.

I Want a Little Dog

One of the most popular dogs in Norway is the Cavalier King Charles Spaniel. It's easy to understand why—they are small and sweet with a soft coat and big eyes.

We think a lot of children would like a sweater with a Cavalier around the yoke. Of course, it would be nicest to have a special dog that the child likes on the sweater. There is nothing to stop you from knitting in a different type of dog if you want. We've included charts for several alternate dogs for you to use. These panels are not as large so you will have to adjust the pattern a little.

If you don't want to juggle so many colors in the dog panel, you can knit the dogs in white and then embroider the brown and black markings on afterwards with duplicate stitch.

CHILDREN'S DOG SWEATER—ROUND YOKE

Sizes (years)	2	4	6
Chest	26 in / 66 cm	28 in / 71 cm	29½ in / 75 cm
Total Length	15 in / 38 cm	17¼ in / 44 cm	19¾ in / 50 cm
Sleeve Length to Underarm	9 in / 23 cm	10¾ in / 27 cm	12¼ in / 31 cm

Yarn and Yarn Amounts

CYCA #2 (sport/baby) PT5 Sport from Rauma (80% wool, 20% nylon, 140 yd/128 m / 50 g). You can substitute yarn that knits to a gauge of 22 sts in 4 in / 10 cm.

Color Suggestions		2	4	6
	566 Medium Blue	200	250	300
	503 Natural White	50	50	50
	532 Chocolate	50	50	50

Needles

U.S. sizes 2-3 and 4 / 3 and 3.5 mm: circulars and set of 5 dpn

Gauge

22 sts and 26 rnds on larger needles = 4 x 4 in / 10 x 10 cm.
Adjust needle sizes to obtain correct gauge if necessary.

Round Yoke—Number of Stitches to Decrease

Sizes (years)	2	(4)	6
Total stitches at beginning of yoke	242	260	282
1st decrease	44 sts, approx. every 5th-6th st	40 sts, approx. every 6th st	40 sts, approx. every 7th st
Sts rem after 1st dec rnd	198	220	242
2nd decrease	36 sts, approx. every 5th-6th st	40 sts, approx. every 5th-6th st	40 sts, approx. every 6th st
Sts rem after 2nd dec rnd	162	180	202
3rd decrease	36 sts, approx. every 4th-5th st	36 sts, approx. every 5th st	40 sts, approx every 5th st
Sts rem after 3rd dec rnd	126	144	162
4th decrease	30 sts, approx. every 4th st	40 sts, approx. every 3rd-4th st	50 sts, approx. every 3rd st
Sts rem after 4th dec rnd*	96	104	112

*After the 4th decrease rnd, make sure the neck opening will fit the person receiving the sweater.

Sleeves

With smaller size dpn and Medium Blue, CO 42 (44, 44) sts. Divide sts onto dpn and join. Knit 8 rnds around in stockinette. Make an eyelet rnd for foldline: (K2tog, yo) around.

Change to larger size dpn and pm at center of underarm. Increase 1 st on each side of marker approx. every 5th rnd until there are a total of 64 (68, 74) sts.
Continue in stockinette with Medium Blue for 7 (8¾, 10¼) in / 18 (22, 26) cm and then work the charted dots and heart panel (12 rnds).

When you reach the point on the chart where the sleeves should be attached, BO 8 sts centered at underarm (= BO 4 sts on each side of marker). Set piece aside and make another sleeve the same way.

Body

The body is worked in the round on a circular ndl. With Medium Blue and smaller circular, CO 146 (156, 166) sts. Join, being careful not to twist cast-on row; pm for beginning of rnd. Knit 8 rnds in stockinette. Make an eyelet rnd for foldline: (K2tog, yo) around.

Change to larger circular and work in pattern following the chart. *At the same time*, pm at each side, moving markers up as you work.

If desired, knit in the dog's name (substituting it for Tassen); see "A Personal Sweater" on page 128. Work 4 (6¼, 8¾) in / 10 (16, 22) cm with Medium Blue between the dog bone and heart panels.

When you've reached the beginning of the yoke, BO 8 sts centered at each underarm (= BO 4 sts on each side of marker). Place sleeves on circular and begin the round yoke.

Yoke

The body and sleeves should now be arranged on larger circular as: back,

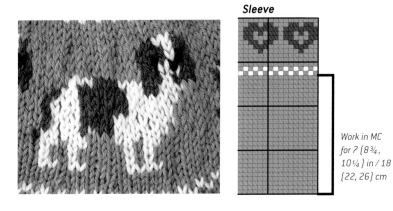

Sleeve

Work in MC for 7 (8¾, 10¼) in / 18 (22, 26) cm

Body

Neckband
4th decrease rnd
3rd decrease rnd

1st decrease rnd

Place sleeves with body on circular here

Work in MC for 4 (6¼, 8¾) in / 10 (16, 22) cm

sleeve, front, sleeve = a total of 242 (260, 282) sts. Continue, following the chart and decreasing as indicated on the chart. The number of sts to be decreased in each decrease round is shown in the table on previous page. Work all decreases as k2tog.

Neckband

Work the neckband following the top panel on the chart. Make an eyelet rnd for the foldline: (K2tog, yo) around. Work 8 rnds in stockinette and then BO loosely. Fold facing to WS and sew down loosely.

Finishing

Seam underarms. Fold facings under and sew down loosely on WS. Weave in all ends neatly on WS.

Blocking

Dampen the sweater in lukewarm water. Gently squeeze out the water. Place a large towel on the floor and put sweater on top. Roll up the towel and press out excess water. Lay the sweater flat on a dry towel or on a sweater drying rack and leave until completely dry.

... or a big dog

Labrador Retriever

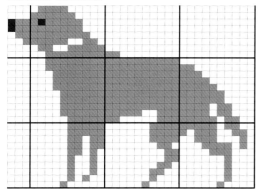

Nova Scotia Duck Tolling

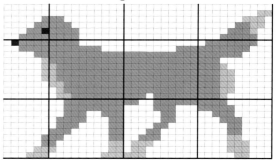

Spitz

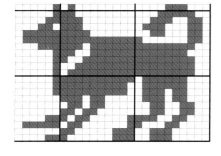

Bird Dog

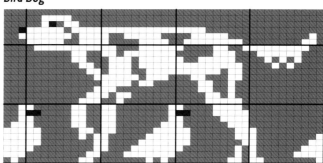

Terrier

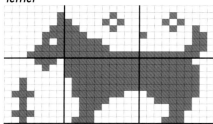

Nova Scotia Duck Tolling Retriever puppies

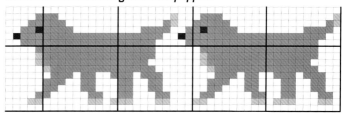

Dachshund

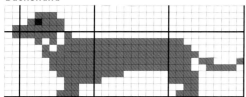

Cavalier King Charles Spaniel

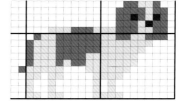

What a Trip!

The inspiration for this sweater came on the car ferry to Andøya. Linn and her family took the spectacular trip along the Helgeland coast over Vest Fjord from Bodø to Å, across Lofoten, and north to Andøya. A fantastic trip that they'll definitely repeat! Linn's father comes from Stokmarknes which is very far north in Norway. The northern climate definitely inspires sweater knitting, and, for that reason, Linn's father modeled the sweater.

The colors of the northern Norwegian landscape are so memorable, especially the sunlight colors as they shift through the clouds and the clear colors that light up towards you.

High, gray mountains with white tops that can be clouds or snow; small red houses at their feet, right at the water's edge. Green, grass-covered hills and nesting cliffs teeming with bird life. The sea, with colorful fishing boats and gulls sweeping overhead. You can go whale watching from several places along the coast, so a whale tail also had to be featured on the sweater. And, of course, fishing streams, a basic source of food in the north.

There were so many motifs that had to be included in this sweater. Fishing boats, gulls, mountains, and reindeer, and finally at the top there had to be the sunset. In the end, the sweater is just as colorful as the landscape it represents.

NORTHERN NORWAY SWEATER—T-SHIRT SHAPING

Sizes	S	M	L	XL
Chest	34¾ in / 88 cm	36¼ in / 92 cm	42½ in / 108 cm	46 in / 117 cm
Total Length	23¾ in / 60 cm	24½ in / 62 cm	26¾ in / 68 cm	28¼ in / 72 cm
Sleeve Length to Underarm	17¾ in / 45 cm	18¼ in / 46 cm	18½ in / 47 cm	19¼ in / 49 cm

Yarn and Yarn Amounts

CYCA #2 (sport/baby) PT5 Sport from Rauma (80% wool, 20% nylon, 140 yd/128 m / 50 g). You can substitute yarn that knits to a gauge of 24 sts and 29 rnds in 4 x 4 in / 10 x 10 cm.

Color Suggestions		S	M	L	XL
	566 Medium Blue	250	250	300	300
	568 Dark Blue	150	150	200	200
	549 Burgundy	50	50	50	50
	563 Plum	50	50	50	50
	547 Red	50	50	50	50
	516 Ochre	50	50	50	50
	590 Green	50	50	50	50
	502 White	100	100	100	100
	504 Light Gray	150	150	150	150
	507 Dark Gray	50	50	50	50

Needles

U.S. sizes 2-3 and 4 / 3 and 3.5 mm: long and short circulars and set of 5 dpn

Gauge

24 sts and 29 rnds on larger needles = 4 x 4 in / 10 x 10 cm.
Adjust needle sizes to obtain correct gauge if necessary.

Sleeves

With Medium Blue and smaller size dpn, CO 46 (48, 50, 52) sts. Divide sts onto dpn and join. Work 12 (12, 18, 18) rnds in k1, p1 ribbing.

Change to larger size dpn and work the sleeve chart, and, *at the same time*, on the first rnd after the ribbing, increase 8 sts evenly spaced around (all sizes). Pm at center of underarm and move it up as you work. Increase 1 st on each side of the marker approx. every 5th (5th, 4th-5th, 4th-5th) rnd until there are a total of 98 (102, 108, 110) sts. Continue in

pattern until the sleeve is 17¾ (18¼, 18½, 19¼) in / 45 (46, 47, 49) cm long or desired length.
Turn sleeve inside out and work 6 rnds in stockinette, increasing 1 st on each side of marker at center underarm on every rnd. BO loosely (= facing). Set piece aside and make another sleeve the same way.

Body

The body is worked in the round on a circular. With Medium Blue and smaller circular, CO 210 (220, 260, 280) sts. Join, being careful not to twist cast-on row; pm for beginning of rnd. Work 18 (18, 24, 24) rnds in k1, p1 ribbing.

Change to larger circular and work the charted pattern. Pm at each side and move up markers as you work.

After completing charted rows for body, follow the sunset chart for your size.
When body measures 23¾ (24½, 26¾, 28¼) in / 60 (62, 68, 72) cm, work the last round:

Body sunset, Sizes S and M

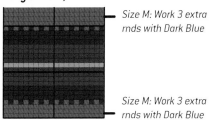

— Size M: Work 3 extra rnds with Dark Blue

— Size M: Work 3 extra rnds with Dark Blue

Body sunset, Sizes L and XL

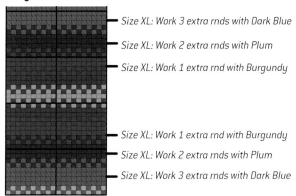

— Size XL: Work 3 extra rnds with Dark Blue

— Size XL: Work 2 extra rnds with Plum

— Size XL: Work 1 extra rnd with Burgundy

— Size XL: Work 1 extra rnd with Burgundy

— Size XL: Work 2 extra rnds with Plum

— Size XL: Work 3 extra rnds with Dark Blue

Body, all sizes, to sunset

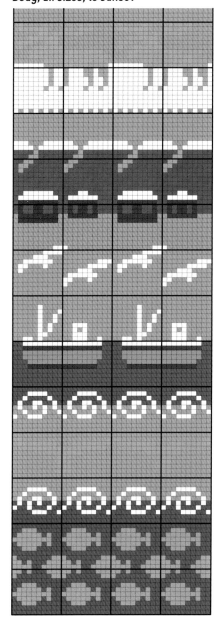

Sleeves, all sizes

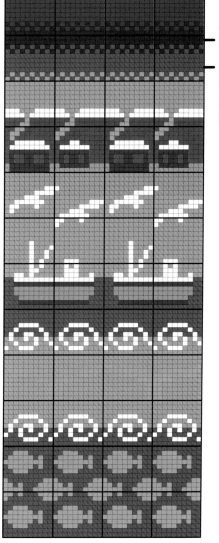

— Size M: Work 1 extra rnd with Plum

— Size XL: Work 2 extra rnds with Plum

— Size M: Work 2 extra rnds with Dark Blue

Size XL: Work 3 extra rnds with Dark Blue

K30 (33, 40, 45), BO 45 (45, 50, 50) sts for front neck, k rem 135 (142, 170, 185) sts.

Finishing
See also Tips and Tricks on page 130.

Seam 30 (33, 40, 45) sts on each shoulder using Kitchener st. Place the sts for the back neck on smaller circular.

Neckband
Baste the front neckline (see sweater photos for shaping) and then work fine zigzag stitching just below basting. Cut away extra fabric from around neck. Use a crochet hook to pick up stitches along the neckline (just below machine stitching) and, with Medium Blue, work 24 rnds in k1, p1 ribbing. BO loosely in ribbing. Fold neckband and sew down loosely on WS, covering cut edges.

Attach Sleeves
Measure the width at the top of the sleeve and then measure half the total sleeve top width down each side for the armhole. Baste line for armhole. Machine-stitch a double row of zigzag stitching on each side of the marking thread. Carefully cut open each armhole between the lines of stitching. Turn sweater body inside out and, working on WS, attach sleeves with fine back stitching. Fold facing over the cut edges and sew down securely.

Blocking
Dampen the sweater in lukewarm water. Gently squeeze out the water. Place a large towel on the floor and put sweater on top. Roll up the towel and press out excess water. Lay the sweater flat on a dry towel or on a sweater drying rack and leave until completely dry.

Warm Hands

This mitten pattern is very easy so you can use any pattern panels you like. As an example, we borrowed some panels from the Northern Norway sweater, but changed out some of the colors. Use the panels you like—wouldn't motifs from the fall sweater or the tulip socks be lovely? We edged our mittens with a short rib but you can, of course, make the ribbing longer. No matter what patterns you choose, these mittens will keep your hands warm and cozy.

NORTHERN NORWAY MITTENS

Sizes
Adult

Finished Measurements
Length: 9½ in / 24.5 cm; width: 4¼ in / 11 cm

Yarn and Yarn Amounts
CYCA #2 (sport/baby) PT5 Sport from Rauma (80% wool, 20% nylon, 140 yd/128 m / 50 g). You can substitute yarn that knits to a gauge of 24 sts and 27 rnds in 4 x 4 in / 10 x 10 cm.

Color Suggestions		Grams
	566 Medium Blue	50
	568 Dark Blue	50
	502 White	50
	504 Light Gray	50

Needles
U.S. sizes 2-3 and 4 / 3 and 3.5 mm: set of 5 dpn

Gauge
24 sts and 27 rnds on larger needles = 4 x 4 in / 10 x 10 cm.
Adjust needle sizes to obtain correct gauge if necessary.

With Medium Blue and smaller size dpn, CO 56 sts. Divide sts onto dpn and join. Work 4 rnds in k1, p1 ribbing.

Change to larger size dpn and knit 1 rnd, increasing 4 sts evenly spaced around = 60 sts. Now work the charted pattern. When you reach the red line on the

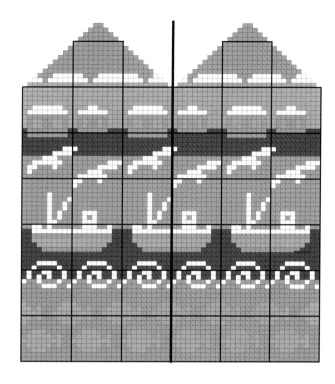

chart, begin the thumb gusset over the marked sts. The rest of the mitten hand continues as set. Because the pattern colors change, feel free to use the colors you are working with for the thumb, as shown on the chart.

At the long red line on the thumb chart, place the 15 thumb sts on a holder. CO 3 sts and then continue with mitten pattern. Shape top as indicated on the chart. Cut yarn and draw end through rem sts; tighten and fasten off.

Thumb
Place the held 15 sts onto dpn and then, with Medium Blue, pick up and knit 7 sts along back of thumbhole = 22 sts total. Knit around until thumb is desired length (about to center of thumbnail) and then shape as shown on the chart. Cut yarn and draw end through rem sts; tighten and fasten off.

Knit the second mitten the same way, reversing position of thumb on palm.

Finishing and Blocking
Weave in all ends on WS. Dampen the mittens in lukewarm water. Gently squeeze out the water. Place a hand towel on the floor and put mittens on top. Roll up the towel and press out excess water. Lay the mittens flat on a dry towel or on a drying rack and leave until completely dry.

High Skies and Bright Colors

During the gray days of autumn, it's a good idea to find some warm red and yellow colors and bring those colors to life on a pretty sweater. We were inspired by fall leaves and the strong contrast they make against clear blue skies, when we're lucky enough to have a nice, clear day.

Fall is the perfect time for picking berries and for filling the freezer with what you can harvest in the woods. Raspberries are great because they ripen in stages, so you can return to your favorite secret berry place and pick more.

Even if there are a lot of panels in this pattern, it is still an easy sweater to knit. There are never more than two colors per round.

Catherine at the Lille Nøste yarn store on Eiksmarka Street in Oslo helped us choose the colors for this sweater and suggested that we substitute double seed stitch for ribbing on the edgings. We agreed that it was an interesting variation. This pattern uses yarn from two mills because we couldn't find all the colors we wanted from just one producer.

AUTUMN SWEATER—ROUND YOKE

Sizes	S	M	L	XL
Chest	36¾ in / 93 cm	39½ in / 100 cm	42¼ in / 107 cm	45¼ in / 115 cm
Total Length	24 in / 61 cm	24 in / 61 cm	28 in / 71 cm	28 in / 71 cm
Sleeve Length to Underarm	19 in / 48 cm	19¾ in / 50 cm	20½ in / 52 cm	20½ in / 52 cm

Yarn and Yarn Amounts
CYCA #3 (DK/light worsted) Falk from Dale of Norway (100% wool, 116 yd/106 m / 50 g)
CYCA #3 (DK/light worsted) Smart from Sandnes (100% wool, 108 yd/99 m / 50 g)
You can substitute yarn that knits to a gauge of 22 sts in 4 in / 10 cm.

Color Suggestions		S	M	L	XL
	3418 Orange (Falk)	350	350	400	400
	2846 Golden Brown (Falk)	100	100	150	150
	4263 Dark Burgundy (Falk)	100	100	100	100
	4137 Wine Red (Falk)	150	150	150	150
	6733 Turquoise (Smart)	100	100	100	100

Needles
U.S. sizes 2-3 and 4 / 3 mm and 3.5 mm: long and short circulars and set of 5 dpn

Gauge
22 sts and 29 rnds on larger needles =
4 x 4 in / 10 x 10 cm.
Adjust needle sizes to obtain correct gauge if necessary.

89

Sleeves

The sleeve length can be adjusted as you work the seed stitch cuff.

With Orange and smaller dpn, CO 48 (48, 52, 52) sts. Divide sts onto dpn and join. Work 12 (18, 26, 26) rnds double seed stitch (see chart).

Change to larger dpn and work following the chart. Pm at center of underarm and move it up as you work. Increase 1 st on each side of the marker approx. every 6th (6th, 6th, 5th-6th) rnd until there are a total of 86 (90, 94, 98) sts.

Work to point on chart indicating the row for joining the sleeves and body. BO 5 sts on each side of the underarm marker (10 sts total). Set piece aside and make another sleeve the same way.

Body

With Orange and smaller circular, CO 204 (220, 236, 252) sts. Join, being careful not to twist cast-on row; pm for beginning of rnd. Work 18 rnds (all sizes) in double seed stitch.

Change to larger circular and work the charted motifs.

NOTE: Sizes S and M begin higher up on the chart than Sizes L and XL.
Pm at each side and move up markers as you work.

When you've reached the start of the yoke, BO 5 sts at each side of underarm marker, on each side of sweater (= BO 10 sts at each side; 20 sts total).

Round Yoke—Number of Stitches to Decrease

Sizes	S	M	L	XL
Total stitches at beginning of yoke	336	360	384	408
1st decrease	30 sts, approx. every 11th st	36 sts, approx. every 10th st	42 sts, approx. every 8th-9th st	39 sts, approx. every 10th-11th st
Sts rem after 1st dec rnd	306	324	342	369
2nd decrease	36 sts, approx. every 8th-9th st	36 sts, approx. every 9th st	36 sts, approx. every 9th-10th st	45 sts, approx. every 8th st
Sts rem after 2nd dec rnd	270	288	306	324
3rd decrease	36 sts, approx. every 7th-8th st	36 sts, approx. every 8th st	36 sts, approx. every 8th-9th st	36 sts, approx. every 9th st
Sts rem after 3rd dec rnd	234	252	270	288
4th decrease	26 sts, approx. every 9th st	28 sts, approx. every 9th st	30 sts, approx. every 9th st	32 sts, approx. every 9th st
Sts rem after 4th dec rnd	208	224	240	256
5th decrease	46 sts, approx. every 4th-5th st	53 sts, approx. every 4th st	60 sts, approx. every 4th st	58 sts, approx. every 4th-5th st
Sts rem after 5th dec rnd	162	171	180	198
6th decrease	22 sts, approx. every 7th st	23 sts, approx. every 7th-8th st	24 sts, approx. every 7th-8th st	30 sts, approx. every 6th-7th st
Sts rem after 6th dec rnd	140	148	156	168
7th decrease	20 sts, approx. every 7th st	24 sts, approx. every 6th st	28 sts, approx. every 5th-6th st	40 sts, approx. every 4th st
Sts rem after 7th dec rnd*	120	124	128	128

*After the 7th decrease rnd, make sure the neck will fit the wearer.

Double Seed Stitch Chart

· = *Purl*

Yoke

The body and sleeves should now be arranged on circular as: back, sleeve, front, sleeve = a total of 336 (360, 384, 408) sts. Continue, following the pattern chart and decreasing as indicated on the chart. The number of sts to be decreased in each decrease round is shown in the table. Work all decreases as k2tog. After the 7th decrease rnd, make sure the neck will fit the wearer.

Neckband

With Orange and smaller circular, work 10 rnds in double seed stitch. BO loosely in seed st.

Finishing

Seam underarms and then weave in all ends neatly on WS.

Blocking

Dampen the sweater in lukewarm water. Gently squeeze out the water. Place a large towel on the floor and put sweater on top. Roll up the towel and press out excess water. Lay the sweater flat on a dry towel or on a sweater drying rack and leave until completely dry.

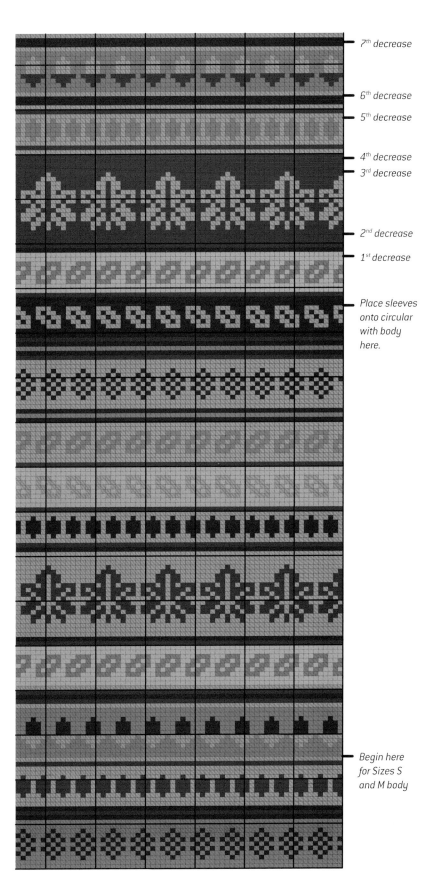

7th decrease

6th decrease

5th decrease

4th decrease
3rd decrease

2nd decrease

1st decrease

Place sleeves onto circular with body here.

Begin here for Sizes S and M body

Give Me a Pillow of Moss

We chose Norwegian Pelsull ("fur" wool) yarn for these soft and pretty pillows. The yarn is available in the loveliest of nature's colors. We think these pillows are at their best in a cabin in the woods or in the mountains.

   The motifs are also taken from the forest. You won't see deer and owls very often, but, if you are patient, you might catch a glimpse of them. If you are very determined and get up early in the morning, you might perhaps see a fairy taking its morning bath in the dewdrops from the leaves of a lady's mantle flower.

FOREST PILLOW COVER WITH FAIRIES

The front and back of the pillow cover are each knitted separately in the round. Each piece is then cut open before the cover is seamed.

Finished Measurements

19¾ x 19¾ in / 50 x 50 cm

Yarn and Yarn Amounts

CYCA #3 (DK/light worsted) Norwegian Pelsull from Hifa (100% wool, 284 yd/260 m / 100 g
OR
CYCA #3 (DK/light worsted) Mitu from Rauma (50% wool, 50% alpaca, 109 yd/100 m / 50 g). You can substitute yarn that knits to a gauge of 20 sts in 4 in / 10 cm.

Color Suggestions		Grams
	Norsk Pelsull 1115 Natural Gray	200
	Norsk Pelsull 1118 Olive Green	100*
	Norsk Pelsull 1103 Cognac	100*

*You only need 50 g but the yarn comes in 100 g skeins.

Needles

U.S. size 4 / 3.5 mm: short circular

Notions

Blunt tapestry needle, pillow form 19¾ x 19¾ in / 50 x 50 cm

Gauge

20 sts and 24 rnds = 4 x 4 in / 10 x 10 cm. Adjust needle size to obtain correct gauge if necessary.

Front

With circular and Natural Gray, CO 100 sts; join, being careful not to twist cast-on row. Work following the chart, and note that the first st of every round is p1. After completing charted rows, the piece should measure approx. 19¾ in / 50 cm. BO loosely. Machine-stitch a double row of fine zigzag on each side of the purl line and cut open between the stitch lines.

Back

With Natural Gray, CO 100 sts. Knit around with only Natural Gray throughout, always purling the first st of the round. When piece measures approx. 19¾ in / 50 cm (same size as front), BO loosely. Machine-stitch a double row of fine zigzag on each side of the purl line and cut open between the stitch lines.

Finishing

Weave in all ends neatly on WS. Fold the pieces with WS facing WS and seam the sides (cut edges) with small back stitching. Seam the top and bottom, leaving an opening for the pillow form at center bottom. Before finishing the pillow, block the cover (see next page).

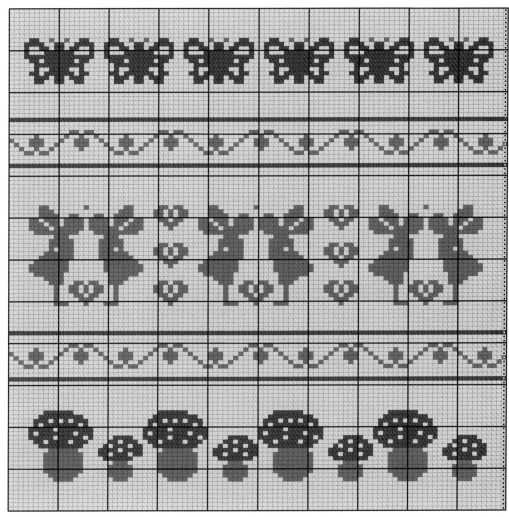

⊙ = Purl

Blocking

With RS facing out, dampen the pillow cover in luke-warm water. Gently squeeze out the water. Place a large towel on the floor and put pillow cover on top. Roll up the towel and press out excess water. Lay the cover flat on a dry towel or on a sweater drying rack and leave until completely dry.

Twisted Edging

While the pillow dries, make the twisted edging. Cut 2 lengths of each yarn color (= 6 strands total), approx. 5¼ yd / 5 meters long (the circumference of the pillow x 2 + a little extra). Knot the strands together at each end and attach one end to a door handle or a similar hook. Begin twisting the strand from the other

end. When the strands feel tightly twisted, grab the center and fold the edging in half. Let the ends twist together. Even out the cord with your fingers and tie a knot at each end.

Finishing Continued

Insert the form into the cover and close the open-ing with RS facing, leaving a small opening for the twisted cord at center bottom. With blunt tapestry needle, sew the cord all around the edge using small overcast sts. The edging will look best if the cord ends meet and neatly overlap at center bottom of cover. Push any overlapping ends into small hole to hide ends and finish seaming.

FOREST PILLOW COVER WITH DEER

The front and back of the pillow cover are each knitted separately in the round. Each piece is then cut open before the cover is seamed.

Finished Measurements
19¾ x 19¾ in / 50 x 50 cm

Yarn and Yarn Amounts
CYCA #3 (DK/light worsted) Norwegian Pelsull from Hifa (100% wool, 284 yd/260 m / 100 g
OR
CYCA #3 (DK/light worsted) Mitu from Rauma (50% wool, 50% alpaca, 109 yd/100 m / 50 g).
You can substitute yarn that knits to a gauge of 20 sts in 4 in / 10 cm.

Color Suggestions	Gram
Norsk Pelsull 1115 Natural Gray	200
Norsk Pelsull 1118 Olive Green	100*
Norsk Pelsull 1107 Lime	100*
Norsk Pelsull 1103 Cognac	100*
+ a small amount of Black for the snouts and eyes	

*You only need 50 g but the yarn comes in 100 gram skeins.

Needles
U.S. size 4 / 3.5 mm: short circular

Notions
Blunt tapestry needle, pillow form 19¾ x 19¾ in / 50 x 50 cm

Gauge
20 sts and 24 rnds = 4 x 4 in / 10 x 10 cm.
Adjust needle size to obtain correct gauge if necessary.

Front
With circular and Natural Gray, CO 100 sts; join, being careful not to twist cast-on row. Work following the chart, and note that the first st of every round is p1. After completing charted rows, the piece should measure approx. 19¾ in / 50 cm. BO loosely. Machine-stitch a double row of fine zigzag on each side of the purl line and cut open between the stitch lines.

Back
With 1115 Natural Gray, CO 100 sts. Knit around with only Natural Gray throughout, always purling the first st of the round. When piece measures approx. 19¾ in / 50 cm (same size as front), BO loosely. Machine-stitch a double row of fine zigzag on each side of the purl line and cut open between the stitch lines.

Finishing
Weave in all ends neatly on WS. Fold the pieces with WS facing WS and seam the sides (cut edges) with small back stitching. Seam the top and bottom, leaving an opening for the pillow form at center bottom. Before finishing the pillow, block the cover (see below).

Blocking
With RS facing out, dampen the pillow cover in lukewarm water. Gently squeeze out the water. Place a large towel on the floor and put pillow cover on top. Roll up the towel and press out excess water. Lay the cover flat on a dry towel or on a sweater drying rack and leave until completely dry.

Twisted Edging
While the pillow dries, make the twisted edging. Cut 2 lengths of each yarn color (= 6 strands total), approx. 5¼ yd / 5 meters long (the circumference of the pillow x 2 + a little extra). Knot the strands together at each end and attach one end to a door handle or a similar hook. Begin twisting the strand from the other end. When the strands feel tightly twisted, grab the center and fold the cord in half. Let the ends twist together. Even out the cord with your fingers and tie a knot at each end.

Finishing Continued
Insert the form into the cover and close the opening with RS facing, leaving a small opening for the twisted cord at center bottom. With blunt tapestry needle, sew the cord all around the edge using small overcast sts. The edging will look best if the cord ends meet and neatly overlap at center bottom of cover. Push any overlapping ends into small hole to hide ends and finish seaming.

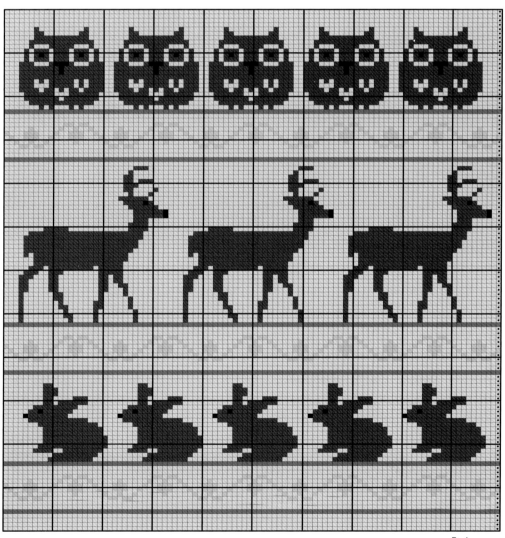

⊡ = Purl

Baa, Baa, Little Lamb

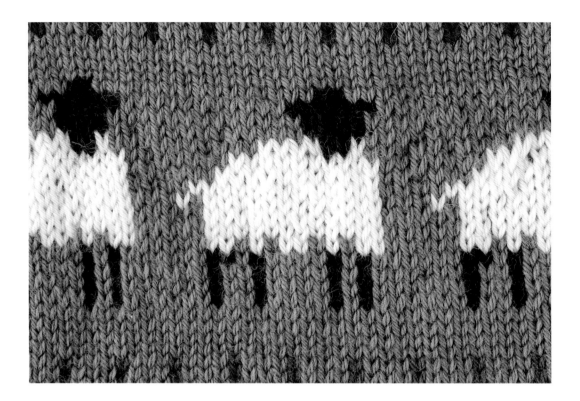

Many children love animals so we've designed this fun barnyard sweater with cows, sheep, hens, and tractors.

Children like fresh, bright colors and our suggestions for this sweater include red, green, white, and brown, with some details in pink. For the smallest size, you can choose sheep or tractors.

The yoke shaping means that only the 6-year size has whole cows. As for all the patterns in this book, the motifs may not come out evenly on all sizes. In this case, there is one tractor not in drivable condition at one side of the sweater. It doesn't matter at all. Children are just as happy and warm even when there is only half a cow or tractor. That's what's great about hen knitting—it doesn't have to be perfect to look good!

We thought it would be extra nice to have a clothes hanger that looks like a hen for the barnyard sweater. If you want to make one, you'll find the instructions further back in the book (see page 126).

CHILDREN'S BARNYARD SWEATER—ROUND YOKE

Sizes (years)	2	4	6
Chest	26 in / 66 cm	28 in / 71 cm	29½ in / 75 cm
Total Length	15 in / 38 cm	17¾ in / 45 cm	19¼ in / 49 cm
Sleeve Length to Underarm	8¾ in / 22 cm	11 in / 28 cm	11¾ in / 30 cm

Yarn and Yarn Amounts

CYCA #3 (DK/light worsted) Falk from Dale of Norway (100% wool, 116 yd/106 m / 50 g)
OR
CYCA #3 (DK/light worsted) Mitu from Rauma (50% wool, 50% alpaca, 109 yd/100 m / 50 g)
You can substitute yarn that knits to a gauge of 22 sts in 4 in / 10 cm

Color Suggestions		2	4	6
	Falk 0020 Natural White OR Mitu SFN 10 Natural	50	50	50
	Falk 4137 Wine Red OR Mitu 6058 Dark Red	100	100	100
	Falk 3072 Chocolate OR Mitu SFN 70 Camel	100	100	150
	Falk 8246 Christmas Green OR Mitu 5340 Green	100	100	150
	Falk 0090 Black OR Mitu SFN 50 Black	50	50	50
	Small amounts Pink for udders and snout of cows			

Needles

U.S. sizes 2-3 and 4 / 3 and 3.5 mm: short circulars and set of 5 dpn

Gauge

22 sts and 26 rnds on larger needles =
4 x 4 in / 10 x 10 cm.
Adjust needle sizes to obtain correct gauge if necessary.

Sleeves

With smaller dpn and Chocolate, CO 42 (44, 44) sts. Divide sts onto dpn and join. Knit 8 rnds around in stockinette. Make an eyelet rnd for foldline: (K2tog, yo) around.

Change to larger dpn and work from correct chart for your size. Pm at center of underarm. Increase 1 st on each side of marker approx. every 5th (6th, 5th) rnd until there are a total of 64 (68, 74) sts.

When you reach the point on the chart where the sleeves should be attached, BO 8 sts centered at underarm (= BO 4 sts on each side of marker). Set piece aside and make another sleeve the same way.

Body

The body is worked in the round on a circular ndl. With Chocolate and smaller circular, CO 146 (156, 166) sts. Join, being careful not to twist cast-on row; pm for beginning of rnd. Knit 8 rnds in stockinette. Make an eyelet rnd for foldline: (K2tog, yo) around.

Change to larger circular and work in pattern following the chart. *At the same time*, pm at each side, moving markers up as you work.

When you've reached the beginning of the yoke, BO 8 sts centered at each underarm (= BO 4 sts on each side of marker). Place sleeves on circular and begin the round yoke.

Yoke

The body and sleeves should now be arranged on larger circular as: back, sleeve, front, sleeve = a total of 242 (260, 282) sts. The number of sts to be decreased in each decrease round is shown in the table on the next page. Work all decreases as k2tog.

Body and Sleeves—4-year size

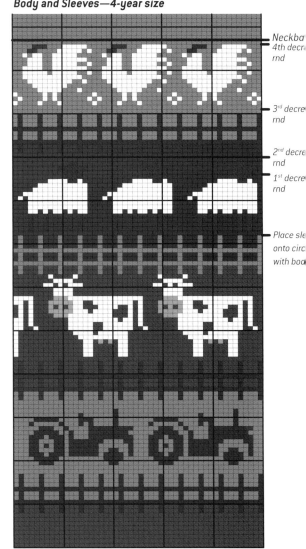

Neckba...
4th decr...
rnd

3rd decre...
rnd

2nd decre...
rnd

1st decre...
rnd

Place sle...
onto circ...
with boo...

Body and Sleeves—2-year size

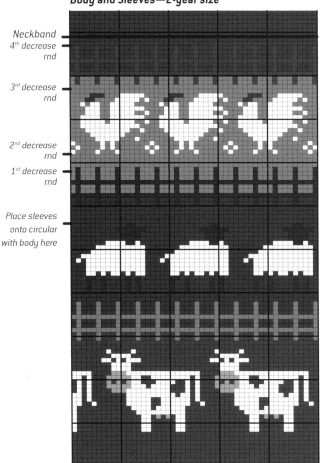

Neckband
4th decrease
rnd

3rd decrease
rnd

2nd decrease
rnd

1st decrease
rnd

Place sleeves
onto circular
with body here

Round Yoke—Number of Stitches to Decrease

Sizes (years)	2	4	6
Total stitches at beginning of yoke	242	260	282
1st decrease	37 sts, approx. every 6th-7th st	36 sts, approx every 6th-7th st	41 sts, approx. every 7th st
Sts rem after 1st dec rnd	205	224	241
2nd decrease	40 sts, approx. every 5th st	40 sts, approx. every 5th-6th st	40 sts, approx. every 6th st
Sts rem after 2nd dec rnd	165	184	201
3rd decrease	36 sts, approx. every 4th-5th st	36 sts, approx. every 5th st	40 sts, approx. every 5th st
Sts rem after 3rd dec rnd	129	148	161
4th decrease	29 sts, approx. every 4th st	40 sts, approx. every 3rd-4th st	51 sts, approx. every 3rd st
Sts rem after 4th dec rnd*	100	108	110

*After the 4th decrease rnd, make sure the neck opening will fit the person receiving the sweater.

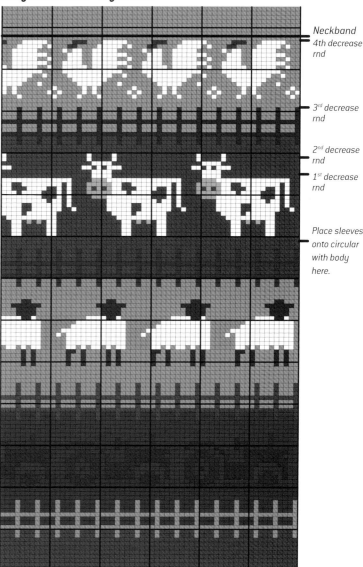

Body and Sleeves—6-year size

Neckband
4th decrease rnd

3rd decrease rnd

2nd decrease rnd

1st decrease rnd

Place sleeves onto circular with body here.

Neckband

With color indicated on chart and larger circular, work 6 rnds in stockinette and then make an eyelet rnd for the foldline: (K2tog, yo) around. Work 7 rnds in stockinette and then BO loosely. Fold facing to WS and sew down loosely.

Finishing

Seam underarms. Fold facings under and sew down loosely on WS. Weave in all ends neatly on WS.

Blocking

Dampen the sweater in lukewarm water. Gently squeeze out the water. Place a large towel on the floor and put sweater on top. Roll up the towel and press out excess water. Lay the sweater flat on a dry towel or on a sweater drying rack and leave until completely dry.

Marvelous Adventure

Cecilie has worked at a nursery school and seen how much fun the children have when they are playing pretend. The nursery school had its own costume box and the children had the most fun when they could dress up for various roles: Superman, Wonder Woman, sorceresses, knights, and ballerinas.

What could be more natural than making little fantasy sweaters for the small princesses and princes in our life? These sweaters feature dragons, white horses, castles, witches, crowns, and swords that will inspire children while they play in their fantasy worlds.

PRINCESS SWEATER—T-SHIRT SHAPING

Sizes (years)	2	4	6
Chest	26 in / 66 cm	28 in / 71 cm	29½ in / 75 cm
Total Length	15 in / 38 cm	16½ in / 42 cm	19¼ in / 49 cm
Sleeve Length to Underarm	10¾ in / 27 cm	11¾ in / 30 cm	13½ in / 34 cm

Yarn and Yarn Amounts

CYCA #2 (sport/baby) PT5 Sport from Rauma (80% wool, 20% nylon, 140 yd/128 m / 50 g). You can substitute yarn that knits to a gauge of 22 sts in 4 in / 10 cm.

Color Suggestions		2	4	6
	561 Light Lilac	250	250	300
	588 Green	100	100	100
	579 Light Pink	50	50	50
	502 Natural White	50	50	50
	528 Beige	50	50	50
	515 Yellow	50	50	50

Needles

U.S. sizes 2-3 and 4 / 3 and 3.5 mm: short circulars and set of 5 dpn

Gauge

22 sts and 27 rnds on larger needles = 4 x 4 in / 10 x 10 cm.
Adjust needle sizes to obtain correct gauge if necessary.

Sleeves

With smaller dpn and Green, CO 42 (44, 44) sts. Divide sts onto dpn and join. Knit 8 rnds around in stockinette. Make an eyelet rnd for foldline: (K2tog, yo) around.

Change to larger dpn and work following chart for size desired. Pm at center of underarm. Increase 1 st on each side of marker approx. every 4th-5th rnd until there are a total of 74 (78, 84) sts.

Continue until sleeve is 10¾ (11¾, 13½) in / 27 (30, 34) cm long or desired length. Turn the sleeve inside out and knit 6 rnds in stockinette for the facing. On each rnd,

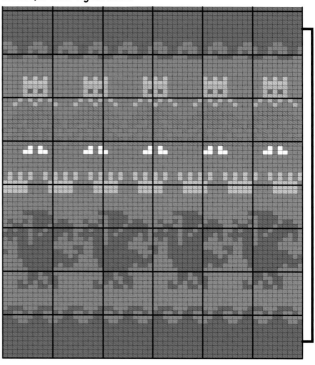

Sleeve, 2- and 4-year sizes

Sleeve rows for 2-year size

increase 1 st before and after the center marker. BO loosely. Set piece aside and make another sleeve the same way.

Body

The body is worked in the round on a circular ndl. With Green and smaller circular, CO 146 (156, 166) sts. Join, being careful not to twist cast-on row; pm for beginning of rnd. Knit 8 rnds in stockinette. Make an eyelet rnd for foldline: (K2tog, yo) around.

Change to larger circular and work in pattern following the chart for your size. *At the same time*, pm at each side, moving markers up as you work.

Adjust the length for 4-year size by adding 10 extra single-color rounds before and after the panels on the body—the heavy line and * at the side of the chart indicate where to add rows.

When the body measures 15 (16½, 19¼) in / 38 (42, 49) cm, work the last rnd as follows: K16 (17, 19), BO 40 (44, 44) sts for front neck, k90 (95, 102) sts.

Finishing

See also Tips and Tricks on page 130.

Seam 16 (17, 19) sts on each shoulder using Kitchener st. Place the sts for the back neck on smaller circular.

Neckband

Place the back neck sts on smaller circular. Baste the front neckline (see sweater photos for shaping) and then work fine zigzag stitching just below basting. Cut away extra fabric from around neckline. Use a crochet hook to pick up stitches along the neckline (below machine-stitching) and, with Green, work the panel for neckband. Make a rnd of eyelets for foldline: (K2tog, yo) around. Knit 8 rnds in stockinette and then BO loosely. Fold neckband and sew down loosely on WS, covering cut edges.

Body, 2- and 4-year sizes

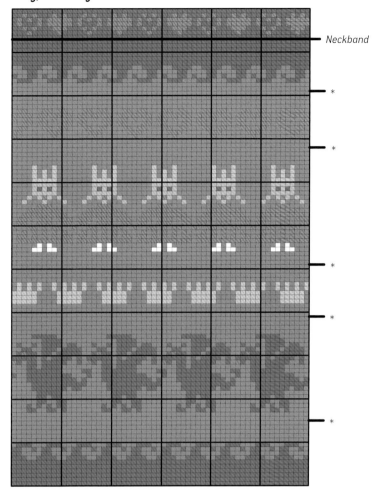

Neckband

*

*

*

*

*

*Add 2 rnds in MC for 4-year size

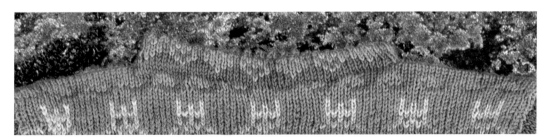

Sleeve, 6-year size

Body, 6-year size

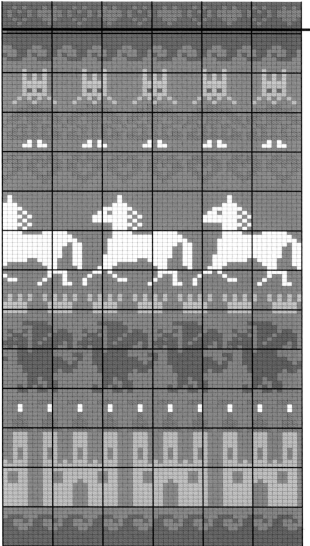

Neckba

Attach Sleeves

Measure the width at the top of the sleeve and then measure half the total sleeve top width down each side for the armhole. Baste line for armhole. Machine-stitch a double row of zigzag stitching on each side of the marking thread. Carefully cut open each armhole between the lines of stitching. With WS of facing on WS of sleeve, attach sleeves with fine back stitching. Fold facing over the cut edges and sew down securely. Fold each sleeve cuff and bottom edge facing along eyelet round and sew facings to WS.

Blocking

Dampen the sweater in lukewarm water. Gently squeeze out the water. Place a large towel on the floor and put sweater on top. Roll up the towel and press out excess water. Lay the sweater flat on a dry towel or on a sweater drying rack and leave until completely dry.

PRINCE SWEATER—T-SHIRT SHAPING

Sizes (years)	2	4	6
Chest	26 in / 66 cm	28 in / 71 cm	29½ in / 75 cm
Total Length	15 in / 38 cm	16½ in / 42 cm	19¼ in / 49 cm
Sleeve Length to Underarm	10¾ in / 27 cm	11¾ in / 30 cm	13½ in / 34 cm

Yarn and Yarn Amounts

CYCA #2 (sport/baby) PT5 Sport from Rauma (80% wool, 20% nylon, 140 yd/128 m / 50 g). You can substitute yarn that knits to a gauge of 22 sts in 4 in / 10 cm.

Color Suggestions		2	4	6
	567 Blue	250	300	350
	582 Light Green	50	50	50
	515 Yellow	50	50	50
	502 Natural White	50	50	50
	588 Green	50	50	50
	528 Beige	50	50	50
	+ a small amount of red for the eyes and mouths			

Needles

U.S. sizes 2-3 and 4 / 3 and 3.5 mm: short circulars and set of 5 dpn

Gauge

22 sts and 27 rnds on larger needles = 4 x 4 in / 10 x 10 cm.
Adjust needle sizes to obtain correct gauge if necessary.

Sleeves

With smaller dpn and Green, CO 42 (44, 44) sts. Divide sts onto dpn and join. Knit 8 rnds around in stockinette. Make an eyelet rnd for foldline: (K2tog, yo) around.

Change to larger dpn and work following chart for size desired. Pm at center of under-arm. Increase 1 st on each side of marker approx. every 4th-5th rnd until there are a total of 74 (78, 84) sts.

Continue until sleeve is 10¾ (11¾, 13½) in / 27 (30, 34) cm long or desired length. Turn the sleeve inside out and knit 6 rnds in stocki-nette for the facing. On each rnd, increase 1 st before

Sleeve, 2- and 4-year sizes

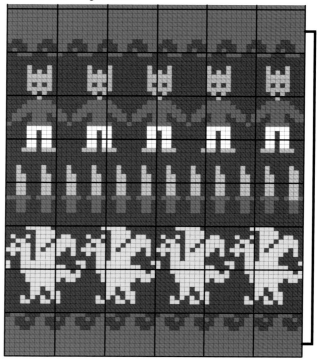

Sleeve rows for 2-year size

and after the center marker. BO loosely. Set piece aside and make another sleeve the same way.

Body, 4-year size

— Neckband

Body, 2-year size

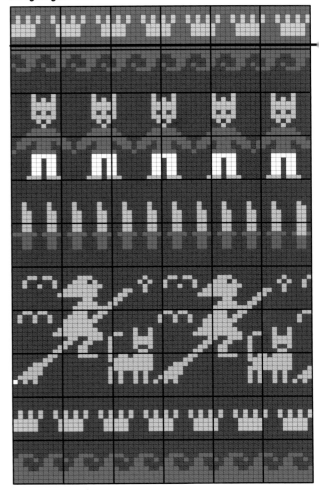

Body

The body is worked in the round on a circular ndl. With Green and smaller circular, CO 146 (156, 166) sts. Join, being careful not to twist cast-on row; pm for beginning of rnd. Knit 8 rnds in stockinette. Make an eyelet rnd for foldline: (K2tog, yo) around.

Change to larger circular and work in pattern following the chart for your size. *At the same time*, pm at each side, moving markers up as you work.

When the body measures 15 (16½, 19¼) in / 38 (42, 49) cm, work the last rnd as follows: K16 (17, 19), BO 40 (44, 44) sts for front neck, k90 (95, 102) sts.

Finishing

See also Tips and Tricks on page 130.

Seam 16 (17, 19) sts on each shoulder using Kitchener st. Place the sts for the back neck on smaller circular.

Neckband

Place the back neck sts on smaller circular. Baste the front neckline shape (see sweater photos for shap-

Body, 6-year size

Neckband

Sleeve, 6-year size

ing) and then work fine zigzag stitching just under basting. Cut away extra fabric above basting around neckline. Use a crochet hook to pick up stitches along the neckline (below machine-stitching) and, with Green, work the panel for neckband. Make a rnd of eyelets for foldline: (K2tog, yo) around. Knit 8 rnds in stockinette and then BO loosely. Fold neckband and sew down loosely on WS, covering cut edges.

Attach Sleeves
Measure the width at the top of the sleeve and then measure half the total sleeve top width down each side for the armhole. Baste line for armhole. Machine-stitch a double row of zigzag stitching on each side

of the marking thread. Carefully cut open each arm-hole between the lines of stitching. With WS of facing on WS of sleeve, attach sleeves with fine back stitching. Fold facing over the cut edges and sew down securely. Fold each sleeve cuff and bottom edge facing along eyelet round and sew facings to WS.

Blocking
Dampen the sweater in lukewarm water. Gently squeeze out the water. Place a large towel on the floor and put sweater on top. Roll up the towel and press out excess water. Lay the sweater flat on a dry towel or on a sweater drying rack and leave until completely dry.

Coffee Klatch

This sweater was inspired by all the cozy things happening in and around cafés. Do you have a café in the neighborhood where you live? Enjoy a cup of coffee or tea; take a break from life's everyday travails. You are not alone; there are many who meet over a good cup of coffee and a tasty cake.

The Norwegian word for klatch—*slabberas*—is, according to the dictionary, "a meeting where one drinks special coffee or tea and chats." Coffee Klatch (*kaffeslabberas*) is also the name of a Danish knitting club on Amager, where the then 27-year-old Susanne Hoffmann collaborated with some Danish artists to publish a knitting, photo, and conversation book. Coffee and knitting is undoubtedly a good combination.

This sweater includes everything we like about café life. Since many mothers in Norway use cafés as public meeting places for mothers' groups, we included a baby carriage—but feel free to change it to a row of muffins or yarn balls in other colors instead. Use the motifs you like to make this your sweater.

The sweater is knitted with Lerke from Dale of Norway, a mixture of wool and cotton. The yarn really lends itself to knitting and the sweater will be soft and lovely.

There are three colors in one round in some of the panels. You can choose to knit with all three or knit with two of the colors and embroider on the least-used one afterwards.

CAFÉ SWEATER—ROUND YOKE

Sizes	S	M	L	XL
Chest	36¾ in / 93 cm	39½ in / 100 cm	42¼ in / 107 cm	45¼ in / 115 cm
Total Length	24 in / 61 cm	24½ in / 62 cm	24½ in / 62 cm	25½ in / 65 cm
Sleeve Length to Underarm	18¼ in / 46 cm	19 in / 48 cm	19 in / 48 cm	19¼ in / 49 cm

Yarn and Yarn Amounts

CYCA #3 (DK/light worsted) Lerke from Dale of Norway (52% Merino wool, 48% cotton, 125 yd/114 m / 50 g
OR
CYCA #3 (DK/light worsted) Mitu from Rauma (50% wool, 50% alpaca, 109 yd/100 m / 50 g).
You can substitute yarn that knits to a gauge of 22 sts in 4 in / 10 cm.

Color Suggestions		S	M	L	XL
	LLerke 2641 Camel or Mitu SFN 73 Beige	250	250	300	300
	Lerke 0020 Natural White or Mitu SFN 10 Natural	200	200	250	250
	Lerke 5752 Slate or Mitu 1992 Steel Gray	150	150	150	150
	Lerke 3046 Light Brown or Mitu 7255 Ochre	100	100	100	100
	Lerke 7215 Turquoise or Mitu 5775 Turquoise	50	50	50	50
	Lerke 3217 Peach or Mitu 0784 Orange	50	50	50	50

Needles

U.S. sizes 2-3 and 4 / 3 mm and 3.5 mm: long and short circulars and set of 5 dpn

Gauge

22 sts and 29 rnds on larger needles = 4 x 4 in / 10 x 10 cm.
Adjust needle sizes to obtain correct gauge if necessary.

Sleeves

With Camel and smaller size dpn, CO 46 (48, 50, 52) sts. Divide sts onto dpn and join. Work 8 rnds in stockinette and then make an eyelet rnd for the foldline: (K2tog, yo) around.

Change to larger size dpn and work 4 (10, 10, 13) rnds in stockinette. Work the heart panel and then continue, following the chart on page 119.

Pm at center of underarm and move it up as you work. *At the same time* as working pattern panels, increase 1 st on each side of the marker approx. every 6th (5th-6th, 5th-6th, 5th-6th) rnd until there are a total of 86 (90, 94, 98) sts. Work to point on chart indicating the row for joining the sleeves and body.

BO 5 sts on each side of the underarm marker (10 sts total). Set piece aside and make another sleeve the same way.

Heart panel

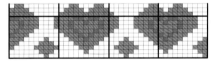

Body

With Camel and smaller circular, CO 204 (220, 236, 252) sts. Join, being careful not to twist cast-on row; pm for beginning of rnd. Work 8 rnds in stockinette and then make an eyelet rnd for the foldline: (K2tog, yo) around.

Change to larger circular and work 6 (10, 10, 18) rnds in stockinette.
Pm at each side and move up markers as you work. Continue, following the chart on page 119.

When you've reached the beginning of the yoke, BO 5 sts at each side of underarm marker, on each side of sweater (= BO 10 sts at each side; 20 sts total).

Round Yoke—Number of Stitches to Decrease

Sizes	S	M	L	XL
Total stitches at beginning of yoke	336	360	384	408
1st decrease	30 sts, approx. every 11th st	36 sts, approx. every 10th st	42 sts, approx. every 9th st	39 sts, approx. every 10th-11th st
Sts rem after 1st dec rnd	306	324	342	369
2nd decrease	36 sts, approx every 8th-9th st	36 sts, approx. every 9th st	36 sts, approx. every 9th-10th st	45 sts, approx. every 8th st
Sts rem after 2nd dec rnd	270	288	306	324
3rd decrease	36 sts, approx. every 7th-8th st	36 sts, approx. every 8th st	36 sts, approx. every 8th-9th st	36 sts, approx.. every 9th st
Sts rem after 3rd dec rnd	234	252	270	288
4th decrease	26 sts, approx. every 9th st	28 sts, approx. every 9th st	30 sts, approx. every 9th st	32 sts, approx. every 9th st
Sts rem after 4th dec rnd	208	224	240	256
5th decrease	46 sts, approx. every 4th-5th st	53 sts, approx. every 4th st	60 sts, approx. every 4th st	58 sts, approx. every 4th st
Sts rem after 5th dec rnd	162	171	180	198
6th decrease	22 sts, approx. every 7th st	23 sts, approx. every 7th st	24 sts, approx. every 7th-8th st	30 sts, approx. every 6th-7th st
Sts rem after 6th dec rnd	140	148	156	168
7th decrease	20 sts, approx. every 7th st	24 sts, approx every 6th st	28 sts, approx every 5th-6th st	34 sts, approx. every 5th st
Sts rem after 7th dec rnd*	120	124	128	134

*After the 7th decrease rnd, make sure the neck will fit the wearer.

Yoke

The body and sleeves should now be arranged on circular as: back, sleeve, front, sleeve = a total of 336 (360, 384, 408) sts. Continue following the pattern chart, decreasing as indicated on the chart. The number of sts to be decreased in each decrease round is shown in the table. Work all decreases as k2tog. After the 7th decrease rnd, make sure the neck will fit the wearer.

TIPS

Some of the decreases fall in the center of a pattern. Try to adjust the decreases so that the motif isn't distorted too much but don't be afraid of small changes either. These little adjustments will make the sweater completely unique.

In the last panel of the yoke, with the open books, it is best if you do not decrease with the stitches outlining the book. Decrease at the center of the book or between the books.

Neckband

With Camel and smaller circular, work the heart panel for the neckband. Work 1 rnd of eyelets for foldline = (k2tog, yo) around. Work 10 rnds in stockinette with Camel and then BO loosely. Fold the facing to WS and sew down.

Finishing

Seam underarms. Fold facings to inside and sew down loosely on WS. Weave in all ends neatly on WS.

Blocking

Dampen the sweater in lukewarm water. Gently squeeze out the water. Place a large towel on the floor and put sweater on top. Roll up the towel and press out excess water. Lay the sweater flat on a dry towel or on a sweater drying rack and leave until completely dry.

Body and Sleeves

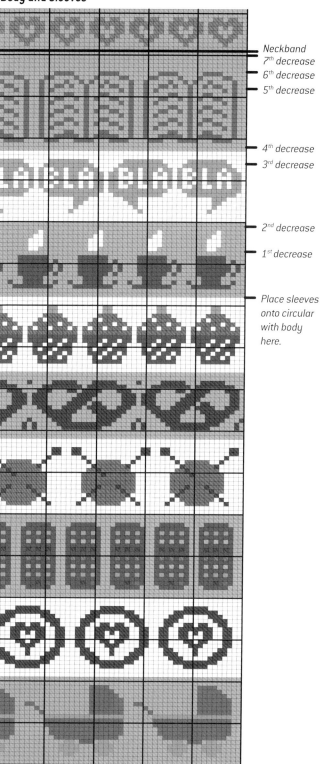

Neckband
7th decrease
6th decrease
5th decrease

4th decrease
3rd decrease

2nd decrease

1st decrease

Place sleeves onto circular with body here.

Hat with Leftover Yarns

This hat provides a great way to use up extra yarn. It's also a good way to see how various colors work together. It's fast to knit and, if you have a lot of colors, the results will always be pleasing. The most difficult aspect is making the hat long enough. Because you don't decrease at the top, it has to be long enough that it won't end up too short when you gather the stitches at the top.

A little advice: When knitting this style of hat, be prepared to knit more than one—our experiences have shown us that this is a hat many people will want!

Finished Measurements
Hat circumference 22 in / 56 cm at lower edge and approx. 10¼ in / 26 cm long after top gathering.

Yarn and Yarn Amounts
Any yarn that knits to a gauge of 22 sts = 4 in / 10 cm. You'll need about 100 g total of several different colors.

Needles
U.S. sizes 2-3 and 4 / 3 mm and 3.5 mm: short circular

Gauge
22 sts and 28 rnds on larger needles =
4 x 4 in / 10 x 10 cm.
Adjust needle sizes to obtain correct gauge if necessary.

Hat
With smaller circular, CO 124 sts. Join, being careful not to twist cast-on row. Pm for beginning of rnd. Work around in k2, p2 ribbing for about 2½ in / 6 cm.

Knit 1 rnd, increasing 4 sts evenly spaced around = 128 sts.

Follow the chart until hat measures 11 in / 28 cm or desired length. The top is finished by gathering rather than shaping with decreases so the hat will

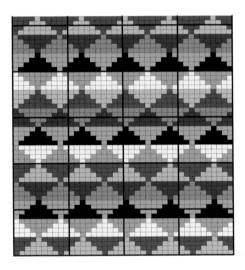

be somewhat shorter once it is finished. Make sure it won't be too short. Cut yarn and draw end through all sts; tighten carefully. Sew the top closed and make a pompom with the same colors as the hat. Attach the pompom securely. Weave in all ends neatly on WS.

Blocking
Dampen the hat in lukewarm water. Carefully squeeze out excess water by rolling it in a towel. Lay hat flat to dry.

TIPS
To make the hat really eye-catching, use colors that contrast well whenever you begin a new panel.

Hen Knitting and Hen Knitting, Mrs. Blom!

This is not traditional hen knitting but we wanted to show how you can make fun garments in the spirit of hen knitting. In this case, we just wanted to combine colors and motifs that we liked together into a scarf. It is not always necessary to have, and we think "hen knitting" also includes all sorts of pattern panels arranged with colorful, joyful motifs.

Maybe we shouldn't use the phrase "hen knitting" so much, but something more like "free knitting" or "playing with pattern and color."

The scarf is doubled and knitted in the round on a short circular. The ends are sewn together in finishing. Depending on whether you want to seam the ends, you can decide if you want to make it like a regular scarf or as a tube scarf.

INCA SCARF IN LOVELY SOFT ALPACA/WOOL

Finished Measurements
Approx. 66 x 17¼ in / 168 x 44 cm. If you want a longer scarf, we suggest that you knit the two red sections longer than shown in the chart. In that case, you will need an extra ball of Wine Red.

Yarn and Yarn Amounts
CYCA #4 (worsted/afghan/aran) Alpakka/Ull from Sandnes Garn (65% alpaca, 35% wool, 109 yd/100 m / 50 g).
You can substitute a yarn that knits to a gauge of 19 sts = 4 in / 10 cm.

Color Suggestions	Grams
4554 Wine Red	100
9581 Dark Green	50
1042 Gray Heather	50
3525 Burnt Orange	50
1088 Charcoal Heather	50
6554 Petroleum	50
2527 Ochre	50

Needles
U.S. size 8 / 5 mm: short circular

Gauge
19 sts and 21 rnds = 4 x 4 in / 10 x 10 cm.
Adjust needle size to obtain correct gauge if necessary.

Scarf
With short circular, CO 80 sts; join, being careful not to twist cast-on row. Pm for beginning of rnd. Work in pattern following the chart. BO loosely when scarf is finished length.

Finishing
Weave in all ends neatly on WS. Use Kitchener st to seam each end. If you want a tube scarf, sew the cast-on and bound-off edges together so that the piece forms a circular tube. If you want a regular long scarf, seam the cast-on and bound-off ends separately. In that case, you'll need to sew each end so that the beginning/end of the round is placed at center back. This is because the edges will be a little uneven if you place the beginning/end of the round at the sides.

Center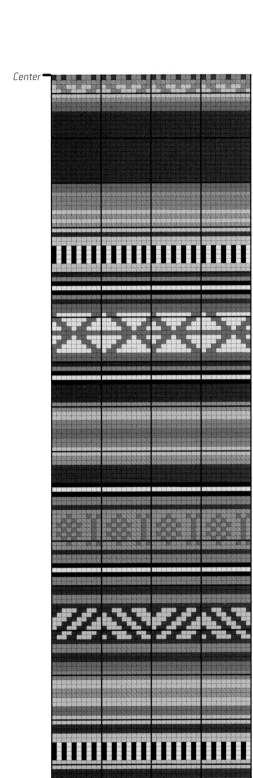

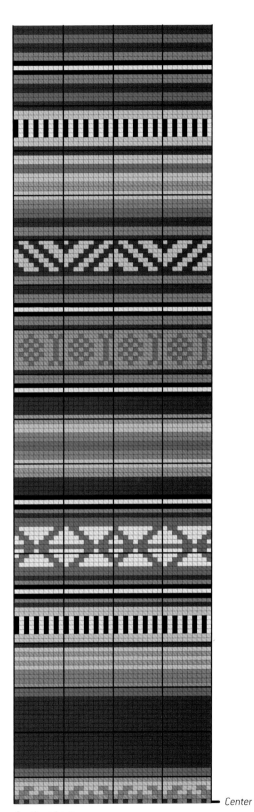 Center

Begin here　　　　　　　　　　　　　　Continue here

125

Clothes Hanger for Hen Knitting

We think it will be fun to knit a clothes hanger with a hen head to hang your sweaters on. It used to be common to cover clothes hangers with fabric or yarn. Besides giving you something to smile about when you open your wardrobe, it's also practical: Garments won't slide off the hangers as easily when you have a "hen cover."

We used flat hangers that you can buy at IKEA, but other clothes hangers with wide hooks can be used instead.

Find a suitable leftover yarn. The cover in the picture was knitted with Lerke from Dale of Norway. If you use a very fine yarn, work with two strands held together.

Measure the outside edges of the hanger. The one we used was approx. 37¾ in / 96 cm. We knitted at a gauge of 22 sts in 4 in / 10 cm so we cast on 210 sts.

Work enough rnds on a circular U.S. 4 / 3.5 mm so that the fabric will cover both the front and back of the hanger. BO all the sts except for approx. 4 sts at the center. CO 4 sts on each side of the 4 center sts and knit a tube with dpn. The number of stitches you'll need depends on how wide the hook is. Knit the tube long enough to cover the whole hook on the hanger. Change to yellow and knit 1 rnd without decreasing. Work k2tog around until all the stitches have been decreased away. This forms the hen's "beak".

The Hen's Comb

With crochet hook and red, ch 6. Turn and work 5 dc in every other ch to make 3 combs. Make the dewlap with ch 3; turn and work 5 dc in the center st.

Sew the comb and dewlap to the tube before pulling it onto the hanger. Seam the "body" on the back of the hanger with Kitchener st.

With yellow, sew on an eye and then make a pupil with black yarn in a simple knot stitch.

Don't forget that hens come in many colors, so play with your yarn colors for more hangers.

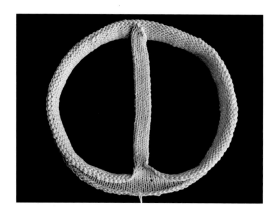
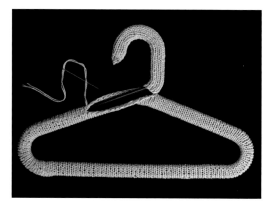

A Personal Sweater

To make a sweater more personal, it is a nice idea to knit in the name of the person you are knitting for, the name of a favorite dog, or a stable or horse name on the front or back of the sweater. You can do this easily by charting the name on graph paper. We provide an alphabet on the next page. Each letter is 7 rounds/rows high. We knitted a simple heart motif on each side of the name but, of course, you can try other motifs that are also 7 rows high.

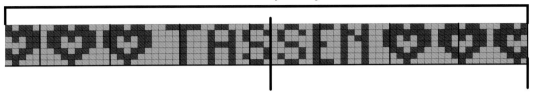

How do you place the name at the center front?

In the following example, there are 150 sts in the body.

Calculate the name

The name "Tassen," for example, has 29 sts with approx. 2 sts on each side of "Tassen," so the name uses a total of 33 sts.

The rest of the panel

A heart is 8 sts, including 1 side st. Take out your calculator and do the math: 150 body sts minus 33 (TASSEN) is 117 sts. To find out how many hearts to knit, divide 117 by 8 = 14.6. That means you can make 14 hearts but will have to add in an extra st between some of the hearts. The name doesn't have to be at the exact center.

The next step is to find the center front

Take out your calculator again and divide 150 sts by 4 = 37.5 sts. That means that it will be approx. 38 sts from the side of the body to the center front.

Finally, figure out how many hearts to knit before beginning the name

Now we subtract 38 sts from half of the name's full count, which is approx. 16 sts, and that leaves 22 sts. Each heart takes 8 sts so we have space for 22 divided by 8 = 2.75 hearts.

Begin at the side marker and knit the first almost complete heart and then 2 hearts; knit in the name, and then continue around with hearts after completing the name. That wasn't so difficult, was it? ☺

Tips and Tricks

Neck openings
Baste a half oval on the front to delineate the neckline shaping (see photo). Machine-stitch a double row of fine zigzag just below the basting. Cut away the excess fabric above the zigzag stitching. With a crochet hook, pick up stitches below the zigzag stitching and then work the neckband following the pattern instructions.

If you don't want to stitch and cut a neckline on a T-shirt shaped sweater, you can form a boat neck. In that case, join fewer stitches than suggested in the pattern for each shoulder.

Joining shoulders with Kitchener stitch

For all of the sweater patterns, we have instructed you to join the shoulders without binding off first. The Kitchener stitch method makes the join invisible and smooth. It is not very difficult but at first it will seem a little awkward. Once you begin, remember that you go through each stitch two times.

Step by Step

1. Begin by threading yarn you will be sewing with into a blunt tapestry needle and then attach the yarn between the two stitch rows that will be joined. Hold the needles on each side of your index finger as shown in the photo.

2. Begin by inserting the tapestry needle into the first stitch on the lower knitting needle PURL-WISE. Go into the first stitch on the top knitting needle KNITWISE.

3. Insert tapestry needle into 1st st of bottom knitting needle KNITWISE and slip stitch off needle. Go into next stitch on lower needle PURLWISE but leave stitch on knitting needle.

4. Insert tapestry needle into 1st st of top knitting needle PURLWISE and slip stitch off needle. Go into next stitch on top needle KNITWISE but leave stitch on knitting needle.

5. Repeat Steps 3-4 until all the stitches have been joined.

Cutting the armholes open

1. Measure half the width of the sleeve top and then measure down the same length from the shoulder down the side of the sweater. Place a marker at base of armhole.

2. With a contrast color yarn, baste down the center of the armhole to the marker. Now you've marked the line that will be cut open. This marked line makes it much easier to reinforce the cutting line with machine stitching.

3. Machine-stitch on each side of the center basting thread. Place the machine foot along the basting so that you will stitch about ¼ in / .5 cm from the basting thread. Using a zigzag (see Step 4 for more information on stitching), stitch on each side of the basting, going around in a U-shape at the top of the shoulder. This might be a little tricky but it will work. At the base of the armhole, stitch back and forth several times for reinforcement.

4. If you have a sewing machine that can make paired zigzag stitches, use it. That way you only have to go once down each side of the basting line. If you don't have that option, use a fine zigzag stitch and stitch down each side of the basting line twice.

5. Remove the basting thread and then carefully cut the armhole open at the center, between the machine-stitched lines. Make sure you don't cut into the top and bottom reinforcement stitching.

6. Attach sleeves: Turn the body inside out and insert the sleeve (right side out) into the armhole so that the facing is above the cut edges on one armhole. Make sure that the sleeve is centered at shoulder and base of armhole. Pin sleeve into place.

7. Use small back stitches to sew in the sleeve securely.

8. Fold the facing over the cut edges and sew down loosely with overcast stitches.

9. Attach the other sleeve the same way.

Shaping in the middle of a pattern

In our designs, we have tried to place any decreases on plain rows between patterns. Sometimes, however, a decrease has to be made in the middle of a motif. Try to work the decreases so that they disturb the motif as little as possible but, at the same time, don't be afraid to have small distortions in the motif. These little pattern shifts will make the sweater uniquely special. See, for example, the picture of the café sweater.

We think it is important for you to try out large and fun motifs even if you think the decreases won't fit in nicely. Check the look as you work and adjust as well as possible. The advantage of knitted garments is that they are so flexible that all will be well in the end.

Stitches and Rows

The row gauge determines how long the garment will be since the charts are based on a specific number of rows. This means that you have to check your gauge in both directions, not just, as usual, the number of stitches across.

Gauge is very important for sizing the finished garment

As an example, we will use a child's sweater, in a 6-year size, which has a gauge of 22 stitches and 26 rows in 4 in / 10 cm. This will make the sweater 29½ in / 75 cm around and 19¾ in / 50 cm long. If you work at a gauge of 24 stitches and 28 rows (tighter knitting), the sweater will be only 27¼ in / 69 cm wide and 18¼ in / 46 cm long. For a Medium adult sweater, the corresponding difference in gauge will mean that sweater won't be a Medium but rather a tight Small.

In each of the patterns, we've listed the gauge and the finished measurements in inches and centimeters. If your garment is not working to that gauge, you can omit or add rows so that the length will be correct.

For that reason, you should knit a gauge swatch before you start the garment to make sure that the garment will fit correctly.

Knitting a gauge swatch in the round on double-pointed needles and in pattern

All the garments in this book are worked in the round, not back and forth, because we think it is difficult to control all the strands when purling and because many knitters work a little more loosely when purling than when knitting. Knitting gauge can also differ between knitting in the round and working back and forth. For that reason, we recommend that you knit a gauge swatch in the round on double-pointed needles.

We also recommend that you knit your gauge swatch with some of the pattern panels you will use in the garment. Our experience tells us that knitting in pattern makes a tighter gauge than knitting in plain stockinette. In other words, you'll need to work a few more rounds in pattern than in single-color stockinette for 4 in / 10 cm in length. It is important to check your gauge as you work, particularly for the length. If your gauge doesn't match that listed in the pattern, then you have to decide whether to add or

omit some rows or panels so that the garment will fit properly. See below for determining how to calculate the length of a panel.

Catching floats

When knitting with two or more colors around, you will have floats on the wrong side with the colors not in use. If there is a long distance between color changes, these floats can become too long. These long floats can easily catch buttons or other objects. To avoid these long floats, you can catch strands as you work. A general rule of thumb is to catch strands at least every 5 stitches.

Measuring the gauge and length of the panels

Gauge is checked by measuring 4 in / 10 cm down the length and across the width of a gauge swatch and then counting the number of stitches across and

rows down. This can best be done when the swatch has been blocked so it will be most like the finished garment. First, use a tape measure to mark off 4 in / 10 cm and mark the length and width with pins. Now you can count the number of stitches and rows. If your gauge is different from that given in the pattern, you can change it by knitting more tightly or loosely with smaller or bigger knitting needles.

In some of the patterns, we suggest that you substitute some of the panels with others for a more personal sweater. If the panel you want to use has fewer or more rows than the one in the pattern, you need to determine how that will affect the length of the sweater. Measurements and calculations might also be necessary if you don't have the correct gauge for the number of rows and need to check how that will affect the total length.

Measuring 4 in / 10 cm of stitches

Measuring 4 in / 10 cm of rows or rnds

Here is how to calculate the length: The length of the panel in inches / centimeters = the number of rounds in the panel/gauge divided by 4 in / 10 cm. For example: The pattern has a panel with 10 rounds that you want to change to a panel with 15 rounds. The gauge is 22 rows in 4 in / 10 cm. In inches, the original panel would be 22 rnds divided by 4 inches = 5.5 rnds per inch. The original 10-round panel would be 1.8 inches long and, at the same gauge, a 15-rnd panel would be 2.7 inches long, or about .9 in longer than the length given in the pattern. In centimeters, 10 cm divided by 22 rnds = .45 cm x 10 rnds = 4.5 cm. The substitute panel would be 15 divided by 22 = .68 x 10 = 6.8 cm. The sweater would then be 6.8 – 4.5 = 2.3 cm longer than the length given in the pattern.

Do I have to knit a gauge swatch?

If you can't wait to begin a garment, and don't mind taking your chances without knitting a gauge swatch, we recommend that you begin with a sleeve. You can measure the gauge once you've worked about 4¼ -4¾ in / 11-12 cm. That way there will be less to rip out if the gauge isn't correct.

Tips for using gauge swatches

If you knitted the gauge swatch in the round, it can easily be sewn into a small bag, pincushion, cell phone or pencil holder, a mug cozy or wrist warmers. You can also use your gauge swatches to practice reinforcing and cutting open (see pages 132-133). Why not join a pile of swatches into a coverlet?

How to block a finished garment

All of the pattern instructions recommend that you block your garment. Blocking is an alternative to light steam pressing and ensures that the stitches will be more even. Blocking also helps if you need to adjust the shaping slightly. We think that blocking is preferable to steam pressing which can easily flatten the garment.

Acknowledgments

Knitters
Siri von Krogh
Kristin Solvang Kvalheim
Gunn Ottersen
Kari Kjønigsen
Margareth Sveinsson

Models
Gro Haram
Anne-Carine Kaurin
Helene Svabø
Rikke Louise M ller
Anna Blom Rian
Runa Marie Bryhn Jacobsen
Ole Gulbrandsen

We would also like to heartily thank all the children who posed for the photos, and their parents.
Ask, Erling, Kaja, Lilly, Maria, Maximilian, Trym, and Hedda Emilie.

A big thank you to the designer Berit Wollebæk Kristoffersen and PtDesign who gave us exclusive permission to use the following panel designs in the book:
Hens in the Farmyard sweater; rose, insect, butterfly, watering can, acanthus, and three-leaf clover panels in the Garden sweater; elves, squid, and seahorses in the Sea sweater; terriers in the children's Dog sweater; giraffes and birds in the Jungle sweater; pastries and coffee cups in the Café sweater; and ducks and sailboats in the Maritime pillows.

Additional Help
Cathrine Hjerpseth Berner, Lille Nøste. Without you we would not have been able to produce this book!
Heidi Janicke Andersen
Helene Svabø
Johan Svabø
Anne-Carine Kaurin
Eugenie and Trygve Husebye
Bjørn Jacobsen
Runa Marie Bryhn Jacobsen
Eirik Bryhn Jacobsen
Chirag and Magdi in Karpe Diem
Morten Andreassen
Jane Camann, Blue Sheep Software LLC Envisionknit
Inger Margrethe Karlsen at Capellen Damm
Sissel Holt Boniface at Capellen Damm

Photograph Credits
Bjørn Jacobsen—Northern Norway Sweater, pages 86 and 101
Michael Angles—Karpe Diem sweater originals from the concert, page 16
Helene Svabø—Karpe Diem sweater originals page 18
Ivana Klavis—Maximilian on the street, page 17
David Wamstad—Helene Sweater, page 12

Last but not least—we had so much fun producing this book but we think that at times our families would have liked to see more of us. Many thanks for being so patient, and also for giving us so much inspiring and encouraging support!